501

Vocabulary Questions

501

Vocabulary Questions

LearningExpress®

NEW YORK

Library of Congress Cataloging-in-Publication Data:
Chesla, Elizabeth L.
  501 vocabulary questions / Liz Chesla.
    p. cm.
  Includes bibliographical references.
  ISBN 1-57685-465-5 (pbk.)
  1. Vocabulary—Examinations, questions, etc. I. Title: Five hundred one
vocabulary questions. II. Title: Five hundred and one vocabulary questions.
III. Title.
  PE1449.C47 2003
  428.1'076—dc21

                                                          2003001224

Printed in the United States of America
9 8 7 6 5 4 3 2 1
First Edition

ISBN 1-57685-465-5

For more information or to place an order, contact LearningExpress at:
    55 Broadway
    8th Floor
    New York, NY 10006

Or visit us at:
    www.learnatest.com

The LearningExpress Skill Builder in Focus Writing Team is comprised of experts in test preparation, as well as educators and teachers who specialize in language arts and math.

LearningExpress Skill Builder in Focus Writing Team

Lara Bohlke
Middle School Math Teacher, Grade 8
Dodd Middle School
Cheshire, Connecticut

Elizabeth Chesla
English Instructor
Coordinator of Technical & Professional Communication
	Program
Polytechnic University, Brooklyn
South Orange, New Jersey

Brigit Dermott
Freelance Writer
English Tutor, New York Cares
New York, New York

Darren Dunn
English Teacher
Riverhead School District
Riverhead, New York

Barbara Fine
English Instructor
Secondary Reading Specialist
Setauket, New York

Sandy Gade
Project Editor
LearningExpress
New York, New York

Melinda Grove
Adjunct Professor, Quinnipiac University and Naugatuck Valley
    Community College
Math Consultant

Noah Kravitz
Curriculum and Technology Specialist
New York, New York

Kerry McLean
Project Editor
Math Tutor
Shirley, New York

William Recco
Middle School Math Teacher, Grade 8
Shoreham/Wading River School District
Math Tutor
St. James, New York

Colleen Schultz
Middle School Math Teacher, Grade 8
Vestal Central School District
Math Tutor
Vestal, New York

Contents

Introduction

A rich vocabulary is both a great asset and a great joy. When you have an extensive vocabulary, you can provide precise, vivid descriptions; you can speak more fluently and with more confidence; you can understand more of what you read; and you can read more sophisticated texts. A good vocabulary can enrich your personal life, help you achieve academic success, and give you an edge over others in the workplace.

Whether you want to improve your vocabulary for a standardized test, learn more effective communication skills to use in the workplace, or be more articulate in social situations, the 501 questions in this book will help you achieve your goal.

How to Use This Book

Each chapter begins with a list of words and their definitions. These are words you can expect to find in newspapers and magazines, in business documents, in textbooks, and on standardized tests like the SAT. The 501 words are divided by theme into 25 chapters. Each chapter has 20 questions to test your knowledge of the words in that chapter. The questions may be multiple-choice, matching, fill in the blank, synonym/antonym, or analogy. In addition, the four "Word Pairs" chapters ask you to complete a crossword puzzle with the chapter's vocabulary words. Answers to each question are provided at the end of each chapter.

The questions increase slightly in difficulty towards the end of the book, but you can complete the chapters in any order you wish. If you prefer one theme over another, you can skip ahead to that chapter. Just be sure to come back and complete each section.

When you are ready to begin, review the word list at the beginning of each chapter. Read each definition carefully. You may find that you do not know the exact meaning of words that you thought were familiar, even if you know the context in which the word is often used. For instance, the phrase *moot point* has come to mean a point not worth discussing because it has no value or relevance. This is a non-standard use of the word but one that has come to be accepted. Moot actually means *debatable* or *undecided*. You may also find that some words have secondary meanings that you do not know.

To help seal the words and their meanings in your memory, try these general vocabulary-building strategies:

1. **Create flashcards.** Use index cards to create an easy and effective study tool. Put the vocabulary word on one side and its meaning and a sample sentence on the other. You can copy the sample sentence from the word list, but you will learn the word faster and remember it better if you create a sentence of your own.

2. **Use the words as you learn them.** The best way to remember what a word means is to *use it*. Make it an active part of your vocabulary as soon as possible. Use the word in a letter to a friend, as you write in your journal, or in your next conversation with a coworker. Share your new words with your best friend, your siblings, or your spouse.

3. **Keep it manageable.** You can't learn 501 new words overnight, and you will only get frustrated if you try to memorize them all at once.

4. **Review, review, review.** After you learn a set of words, remember to review those words regularly. If you simply keep moving forward with new words without stopping to review everything you have already learned, much of your effort will be in vain. Repetition is the key to mastery, especially with vocabulary. The more you review the words and their meanings and the more you use them, the more quickly and permanently they will become part of your vocabulary.

You can use this book to review as often as you like. Review the word list periodically, and give yourself the opportunity to answer each question more than once. Instead of writing in this book, write all of your answers on a separate piece of paper. If you prefer to write in the book, mark your answers lightly in pencil so that you can erase your answers and use the 501 questions for review a few months or years down the road.

Congratulations on taking these very important steps toward building a better vocabulary. Enjoy!

501
Vocabulary Questions

1

It's Not What You Say, But How You Say It

Have you ever been severely *remonstrated* by an authority figure for doing something you shouldn't have? Have you ever embarrassed yourself by committing a *solecism* during a formal occasion? As we communicate with one another, we use words as a means of expression. The words in this chapter describe different things we might say and how we might say them. You can find the answers to each question in this section at the end of the chapter.

Word List

bombastic (bom·'bas·tik) *adj.* speaking pompously, with inflated self-importance. *Ahmed was shocked that a renowned and admired humanitarian could give such a bombastic keynote address.*

censure ('sen·shŭr) *n.* an expression of strong criticism or disapproval; a rebuke or condemnation. *After the Senator was found guilty of taking bribes, Congress unanimously agreed to censure him.*

derisive (di·'rī·siv) *adj.* scornful, expressing ridicule; mocking, jeering. *In order to ensure a positive environment, derisive comments were forbidden in the classroom.*

disparage (di·'spar·ij) *v.* to speak of in a slighting or derogatory way; to belittle. *Comedians often disparage politicians as part of their comedic routines.*

effusive (i·'fyoo·siv) *adj.* expressing emotions in an unrestrained or excessive way; profuse, overflowing, gushy. *Anne's unexpected effusive greeting made Tammy uncomfortable.*

eloquent ('el·ŏ·kwĕnt) *adj.* expressing strong emotions or arguments in a powerful, fluent, and persuasive manner. *Abraham Lincoln's Gettysburg Address is considered one of the most eloquent speeches ever given by a U.S. president.*

gainsay ('gayn·say) *v.* to deny, contradict, or declare false; to oppose. *Petra would gainsay all accusations made against her.*

harangue (ha·'rang) *n.* a long, often scolding or bombastic speech; a tirade. *Members of the audience began to get restless during the senator's political harangue.*

importune (im·por·'toon) *v.* 1. to ask incessantly, make continuous requests. 2. to beg persistently and urgently. *Children can't help but importune during the holidays, constantly nagging for the irresistible toys they see advertised on television.*

malapropism ('mal·ă·prop·iz·ĕm) *n.* comical misuse of words, especially those that are similar in sound. *The politician's malapropisms may make us laugh, but they will not win our votes.*

mince (mins) *v.* 1. to cut into very small pieces. 2. to walk or speak affectedly, as with studied refinement. 3. to say something more delicately or indirectly for the sake of politeness or decorum. *Please don't mince your words—just tell me what you want to say.*

opprobrious (ŏ·′proh·bri·ŭs) *adj.* 1. expressing contempt or reproach; scornful, abusive. 2. bringing shame or disgrace. *It was inappropriate to make such opprobrious remarks in front of everybody.*

oxymoron (oks·i·′moh·rŏn) *n.* a figure of speech containing a seemingly contradictory combination of expressions, such as *friendly fire. The term "non-working mother" is a contemptible oxymoron.*

platitude (′plat·i·tood) *n.* a trite or banal statement, especially one uttered as if it were new. *Matthew offered me several platitudes but no real advice.*

remonstrate (ri·′mon·strayt) *v.* 1. to say or plead in protest, objection, or opposition. 2. to scold or reprove. *The children remonstrated loudly when their mother told them they couldn't watch that movie.*

repartee (rep·ăr·′tee) *n.* 1. a quick, witty reply. 2. the ability to make witty replies. *He wasn't expecting such a sharp repartee from someone who was normally so quiet.*

sardonic (sahr·′don·ik) *adj.* sarcastic; mocking scornfully. *I was hurt by his sardonic reply.*

sententious (sen·′ten·shŭs) *adj.* 1. expressing oneself tersely; pithy. 2. full of maxims and proverbs offered in a self-righteous manner. *I was looking for your honest opinion, not a sententious reply.*

solecism (′sol·ĕ·siz·ĕm) *n.* 1. a mistake in the use of language. 2. violation of good manners or etiquette; impropriety. *Frank's solecism caused his debate team much embarrassment.*

voluble (′vol·yŭ·bĕl) *adj.* 1. talking a great deal and with great ease; language marked by great fluency; rapid, nimble speech. 2. turning or rotating easily on an axis. *Your new spokesperson is very voluble and clearly comfortable speaking in front of large audiences.*

Read the following sentences carefully. Decide which word best describes what is being said and circle the letter of the correct answer. (If you do not own this book, please write your answers on a separate piece of paper.)

1. "Bundle up," said Aunt Margaret. "I don't want you getting sick and coming down with <u>ammonia</u>."

   The underlined word is a(n)
   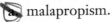
   a. malapropism.
   b. solecism.
   c. oxymoron.
   d. harangue.

2. Jack pleaded, "Can I go on the rollercoaster one more time, Mom? Please? I really, really want to. Pretty please? I'll do extra chores this week. Please?"

   This little boy is
   a. gainsaying his mother.
   b. importuning his mother.
   c. disparaging his mother.
   d. censuring his mother.

3. "You are hopeless! I cannot believe your files are in such disorder," the irritable supervisor shouted.

   This remark is
   a. effusive.
   b. sententious.
   c. bombastic.
   d. opprobrious.

4. "Come on, Mom! You're not being fair! Why can't I stay out until midnight just like my friends? I'm old enough," stated Marissa emphatically.

   This teenager is
   a. remonstrating her mother.
   b. importuning her mother.
   c. gainsaying her mother.
   d. being sententious.

5. "Oh, wow! I just can't believe it! I'm so excited! This is the best thing ever! I am very, very happy," the new homeowner declared.

This remark is
a. bombastic.
b. eloquent.
c. effusive.
d. sardonic.

6. The cranky old coach yelled, "You call that a pitch? I've seen rookies with better aim."

This remark is
a. derisive.
b. sententious.
c. voluble.
d. effusive.

7. "We'd only just met the host when Kenny told her that her house desperately needed a makeover," Janine said. "I was so embarrassed!"

Kenny's comment was a(n)
a. malapropism.
b. solecism.
c. oxymoron.
d. platitude.

8. "Well, son, I've got news for you: You win some, you lose some. Besides, it's not whether you win or lose that counts. It's how you play the game," my old-fashioned dad said.

This remark is
a. sententious.
b. sardonic.
c. eloquent.
d. derisive.

9. "They've labeled the poster an <u>authentic reproduction</u>," the antique dealer said. "That's like calling a book on the bestseller list a <u>new classic</u>."

    The underlined words are examples of a(n)
    a. malapropism.
    b. oxymoron.
    c. platitude.
    d. repartee.

10. "No, that's not how it happened," the honor student said. "Julianna is lying. Winston didn't steal her idea; she took it from him."

    This speaker is
    a. censuring.
    b. disparaging.
    c. gainsaying.
    d. mincing.

Read the following sentences carefully. Decide which of the words from the following list best fills the blank in the sentence. Write your answer in the blank. (If you do not own this book, please write your answer on a separate piece of paper.)

bombastic   mince

censure   platitude

disparage   repartee

eloquent   sardonic

harangue   voluble

11. Darlene found that Jonathan's remarks ___disparage___(ed) her so much that their relationship was at stake. His critical comments were unkind.

12. When he discovered the error, Chesterton lashed out at Watkins. His ___harangue___ lasted for several minutes and shocked everyone in my department!

13. ABC Paper has been polluting our river for the last 20 years and has been keeping it from the public. This is not just wrong, it's criminal. ABC Paper is guilty of unforgivable sins against the environment and against the people of our state and deserves the most severe _censure_.

14. Because she is so _voluble_, she has no trouble meeting new people or talking in front of a crowd.

15. I wish Edna would be more straightforward. She's always _mince_(ing) her words, as if she is afraid she will hurt my feelings.

16. What a(n) _eloquent_ essay! It is forceful and fluent with powerful and precise word choice throughout the text.

17. Caleb's reply was _sardonic_, as usual. He can't seem to say anything without mockery.

18. Titus tried to insult Isabel, but she tactfully deflected the insult with a witty _repartee_.

19. She thought she was offering some real advice, but all she could give me was some _platitude_(s) like "tomorrow's another day" and "good things come to those who wait."

20. How could our humble, soft-spoken president make such a _bombastic_ statement to the newcomer in the group?

Answers

1. **a.** A *malapropism* is the comical misuse of words, especially those similar in sound. Here, the speaker says, "ammonia" instead of "pneumonia."

2. **b.** To *importune* is to ask incessantly or beg persistently.

3. **d.** An *opprobrious* remark is one that is scornful and expresses contempt.

4. **a.** To *remonstrate* is to say or plead in protest or objection. *Remonstrate* can also mean *to scold* or *reprove*.

5. **c.** An *effusive* remark expresses emotions in an unrestrained or excessive way.

6. **a.** A *derisive* comment expresses scorn and ridicules or mocks something or someone.

7. **b.** A *solecism* is a mistake in the use of language or a violation of good manners or etiquette.

8. **a.** A *sententious* reply is one that is full of maxims and proverbs offered in a self-righteous manner. *Sententious* can also mean *expressing oneself tersely*.

9. **b.** An *oxymoron* is a figure of speech containing a seemingly contradictory combination of words. *Authentic reproduction* and *new classic* are oxymorons.

10. **c.** To *gainsay* is to deny, contradict, or declare false; to oppose.

11. To *disparage* is to belittle, to speak of in a derogatory way.

12. A *harangue* is a tirade; a long, scolding or bombastic speech.

13. A *censure* is a rebuke or expression of strong criticism and disapproval.

14. A *voluble* person talks a great deal and with immense ease.

15. To *mince* means to say something more delicately or indirectly for the sake of politeness or decorum. It can also mean to chop into very small pieces or to walk or speak affectedly.

16. *Eloquent* means expressing strong emotions or arguments in a powerful, fluent, and persuasive manner.

17. *Sardonic* means sarcastic, mocking scornfully.

18. A *repartee* is a quick, witty reply or the ability to make such replies.

19. A *platitude* is a trite or banal statement, especially one uttered as if it were new.

20. *Bombastic* means speaking pompously, with inflated self-importance.

2

Word Pairs I

Have you ever felt *ambivalent* or *irresolute*? Did you ever smell something *noisome* or *noxious*? These words are almost exactly the same in meaning, and they are called *word pairs*. This is the first of four chapters of word pairs. Each word pair chapter contains ten sets of synonyms.

Word List

ambivalent (am·ˈbiv·ă·lĕnt) *adj.* having mixed or conflicting feelings about a person, thing, or situation; uncertain. *She was ambivalent about the proposal for the shopping center because she understood the arguments both for and against its construction.*

ephemeral (i·ˈfem·ĕ·răl) *adj.* lasting only a very short time; transitory. *Numerous ephemeral ponds and pools can be found in the desert during the rainy season.*

garrulous (ˈgar·ŭ·lŭs) *adj.* talkative. *Andrew had the unfortunate luck of being seated next to a garrulous young woman for his 12-hour flight.*

inchoate (in·ˈkoh·it) *adj.* 1. just begun; in an initial or early stage of development; incipient. 2. not yet fully formed; undeveloped, incomplete. *During the inchoate stage of fetal growth, it is difficult to distinguish between a cow, a frog, and a human; it is not until they mature that the developing embryos take on the characteristics of their own particular species.*

irk (urk) *v.* to annoy, irritate, or vex. *Teenagers are continually irked by their parents—and vice versa.*

irresolute (i·ˈrez·ŏ·loot) *adj.* feeling or showing uncertainty; hesitant, indecisive. *Sandra is still irresolute, so if you talk to her, you might help her make up her mind.*

loquacious (loh·ˈkway·shŭs) *adj.* talkative, garrulous. *The loquacious woman sitting next to me on the six-hour flight talked the entire time.*

mitigate (ˈmit·ĭ·gayt) *v.* 1. to make less intense or severe. 2. to moderate the force or intensity of, soften; diminish, alleviate. *The unusual extenuating circumstances mitigated her punishment.*

nascent (ˈnas·ĕnt) *adj.* coming into existence, emerging. *The nascent movement gathered strength quickly and soon became a nationwide call to action.*

noisome (ˈnoi·sŏm) *adj.* 1. offensive, foul, especially in odor; putrid. 2. harmful, noxious. *What a noisome odor is coming from that garbage can!*

noxious (ˈnok·shŭs) *adj.* unpleasant and harmful, unwholesome. *The noxious smell drove everyone from the room.*

palliate (ˈpal·i·ayt) *v.* 1. to make something less intense or severe; mitigate, alleviate; to gloss over, put a positive spin on. 2. to provide relief from pain, relieve the symptoms of a disease or disorder. *The governor tried to palliate* *his malfeasance, but it soon became clear that he would not be able to prevent a scandal.*

rapacious (ră·ˈpay·shŭs) *adj.* excessively greedy and grasping (especially for money); voracious, plundering. *The rapacious general ordered his soldiers to pillage the town.*

sordid (ˈsor·did) *adj.* 1. dirty, wretched, squalid. 2. morally degraded. *This sordid establishment should be shut down immediately.*

squalid (ˈskwol·id) *adj.* 1. filthy and wretched. 2. morally repulsive, sordid. *The housing inspectors noted such deplorable and squalid living conditions in the decrepit building on Water Street that they were forced to evacuate the tenants.*

stoical (ˈstoh·i·kăl) *adj.* seemingly unaffected by pleasure or pain; indifferent, impassive. *He remained stoical as his wife told him she was leaving.*

stolid (ˈstol·id) *adj.* not feeling or showing emotion, impassive; not easily aroused or excited. *Maxine is a very stolid person, so it is very difficult to tell how she feels.*

transient (ˈtran·zhĕnt) *adj.* lasting only a very short time; fleeting, transitory, brief. *Their relationship was transient, but profound.*

vex (veks) *v.* 1. to annoy, irritate. 2. to cause worry to. *I was completely vexed by his puerile behavior.*

voracious (voh·ˈray·shŭs) *adj.* excessively greedy, rapacious; having a great appetite for something, devouring greedily. *I have always been a voracious reader, consuming dozens of books every month.*

Crossword Puzzle Directions

In this puzzle, each clue is offered twice, once for each word in the word pair. Read the definition provided in the clue and determine which two words share that meaning. Then, determine which of those synonyms fits in the designated crossword squares.

Word Pairs I Crossword Puzzle

ACROSS

   22.   to annoy, irritate (paired with 30 down)

   23.   not showing emotion (paired with 38 down)

   26.   talkative, chatty (paired with 24 down)

   29.   excessively greedy (paired with 31 down)

   32.   unsure, undecided (paired with 25 down)

   33.   dirty, filthy, wretched (paired with 27 down)

   34.   brief, lasting only a short time (paired with 28 down)

   37.   to make less intense or severe (paired with 40 across)

   39.   foul, unhealthy (paired with 21 down)

   40.   to make less intense or severe (paired with 37 across)

DOWN

   21.   foul, unhealthy (paired with 39 across)

   24.   talkative, chatty (paired with 26 across)

   25.   unsure, undecided (paired with 32 across)

   27.   dirty, filthy, wretched (paired with 33 across)

   28.   brief, lasting only a short time (paired with 34 across)

   30.   to annoy, irritate (paired with 22 across)

   31.   excessively greedy (paired with 29 across)

   35.   just beginning, in its earliest stages (paired with 36 down)

   36.   just beginning, in its earliest stages (paired with 35 down)

   38.   not showing emotion (paired with 23 across)

Answers

The following words are *word pairs:*
ambivalent, irresolute
ephemeral, transient
garrulous, loquacious
inchoate, nascent
irk, vex
mitigate, palliate
noisome, noxious
rapacious, voracious
sordid, squalid
stoical, stolid

Across

22. To *vex* means to annoy or irritate; *irk*.

23. *Stoical* means seemingly unaffected by pleasure or pain; indifferent or impassive. A stoical person, like a *stolid* person, would not show emotion.

26. *Garrulous* means talkative, chatty; *loquacious*.

29. *Rapacious* means excessively greedy and grasping, *voracious*.

32. *Irresolute* means feeling or showing uncertainty; hesitant, indecisive, or *ambivalent*.

33. *Sordid* means dirty, wretched, *squalid*; it can also mean morally degraded.

34. *Transient* means lasting only a very short time; fleeting, transitory, brief; *ephemeral*.

37. To *palliate* means to make something less intense or severe, to *mitigate* or alleviate; to put a positive spin on. It can also mean to provide relief from pain or from symptoms of a disease.

39. *Noisome* means offensive, foul, especially in odor; harmful or *noxious*.

40. To *mitigate* is to make less intense or severe; to moderate the force or intensity of something; alleviate, *palliate*.

Down

21. *Noxious* means unpleasant and harmful; unwholesome, *noisome*.

24. *Loquacious* means talkative; *garrulous*.

25. *Ambivalent* means having mixed or conflicting feelings about something; uncertain, *irresolute*.

27. *Squalid* means filthy, wretched; morally repulsive, *sordid*.

28. *Ephemeral* means lasting only a very short time; *transient*.

30. *Irk* means to annoy, irritate; *vex*.

31. *Voracious* means excessively greedy, having a great appetite for something, *rapacious*.

35. *Inchoate* means just begun, in an initial or early stage of development; *nascent*.

36. *Nascent* means just coming into existence, emerging; *inchoate*.

38. *Stolid* means not feeling or showing emotion; impassive, *stoical*.

3

Personality Traits and Attitudes I

Are you *personable* or *petulant*? *Perfidious* or *punctilious*? The 20 words in this chapter identify some of the characteristics that describe who we are and how we behave.

Word List

blithe (blīth) *adj.* lighthearted, casual, and carefree. *Rachel's blithe attitude toward spending money left her penniless and in debt.*

bumptious ('bump·shŭs) *adj.* arrogant, conceited. *The bumptious man could not stop talking about himself or looking in the mirror.*

capricious (kă·'prish·ŭs) *adj.* impulsive, whimsical, and unpredictable. *Robin Williams, the comedian, demonstrates a most capricious nature even when he is not performing.*

churlish ('chur·lĭsh) *adj.* ill-mannered, boorish, rude. *Angelo's churlish remarks made everyone at the table uncomfortable and ill at ease.*

circumspect ('sur·kŭm·spekt) *adj.* cautious, wary, watchful. *The captain was circumspect as he guided the boat through the fog.*

craven ('kray·vĕn) *adj.* cowardly. *"This craven act of violence will not go unpunished," remarked the police chief.*

diffident ('dif·i·dĕnt) *adj.* lacking self-confidence; shy and timid. *Alan's diffident nature is often misinterpreted as arrogance.*

gregarious (grĕ·'gair·i·ŭs) *adj.* 1. seeking and enjoying the company of others; sociable. 2. tending to form a group with others of the same kind. *John was a gregarious fellow who always had fun at social events.*

irascible (i·'ras·ĭ·bĕl) *adj.* irritable, easily aroused to anger; hot tempered. *Her irascible temperament caused many problems with the staff at the office.*

overweening (oh·vĕr·'wee·ning) *adj.* 1. presumptuously arrogant, overbearing. 2. excessive, immoderate. *I quit because I couldn't stand to work for such an overweening boss.*

perfidious (pĕr·'fid·i·ŭs) *adj.* treacherous, dishonest; violating good faith, disloyal. *The perfidious knight betrayed his king.*

personable ('pur·sŏ·nă·bĕl) *adj.* pleasing in appearance or manner; attractive. *Sandra is personable and well-liked by her peers.*

petulant ('pech·u·lănt) *adj.* peevish; unreasonably or easily irritated or annoyed. *The pouting and sulking child could only be described as petulant.*

pretentious (pri·'ten·shŭs) *adj.* showy, pompous, putting on airs. *Hannah thinks that being pretentious will make people like her, but she is sorely mistaken.*

puerile (ˈpyoo·ĕ·rĭl) *adj.* 1. childish, immature. 2. suitable only for children; belonging to or of childhood. *Andrew is a remarkably successful businessman for someone so puerile.*

punctilious (pungk·ˈtil·i·ŭs) *adj.* very conscientious and precise; paying great attention to details or trivialities, especially in regard to etiquette. *Kira is as punctilious in her personal affairs as she is in the workplace.*

sagacious (să·ˈgay·shŭs) *adj.* having or showing sound judgment; perceptive, wise. *My sagacious uncle always gives me good, sound advice.*

sanguine (ˈsang·gwin) *adj.* 1. confidently cheerful, optimistic. 2. of the color of blood; red. *People are drawn to her because of her sanguine and pleasant nature.*

saturnine (ˈsat·ŭr·nīn) *adj.* gloomy, dark, or sullen. *The saturnine child sulked for hours.*

surly (ˈsur·lee) *adj.* bad-tempered, gruff, or unfriendly in a way that suggests menace. *Emily received a surly greeting from the normally cheerful receptionist.*

Choose the answer that is the best response for each question below. If you do not own this book, please write your answers on a separate piece of paper.

41. Which of the following traits is *most* desirable in a roommate?
    a. bumptious
    b. personable
    c. pretentious
    d. puerile

42. Which of the following traits is *least* desirable in a roommate?
    a. diffident
    b. gregarious
    c. sanguine
    d. surly

43. Which kind of person would most likely make the best waiter?
    a. someone who is blithe
    b. someone who is overweening
    c. someone who is perfidious
    d. someone who is punctilious

44. Which kind of person would most likely make the best spy?
    a. someone who is capricious
    b. someone who is craven
    c. someone who is perfidious
    d. someone who is sagacious

45. Which kind of person would most likely make the best judge?
    a. someone who is diffident
    b. someone who is sagacious
    c. someone who is sanguine
    d. someone who is saturnine

46. Which kind of person would most likely make the best security guard?
    a. someone who is bumptious
    b. someone who is circumspect
    c. someone who is gregarious
    d. someone who is perfidious

47. Which kind of person would most likely be the best companion when you are feeling sad?
   a. someone who is bumptious
   b. someone who is irascible
   c. someone who is puerile
   d. someone who is sanguine

48. Which character trait would you *least* like to see in a soldier?
   a. craven
   b. overweening
   c. pretentious
   d. surly

49. Which character trait would you *least* like to see in a judge?
   a. capricious
   b. circumspect
   c. personable
   d. punctilious

50. Which character trait would you *least* like to see in a supervisor?
   a. blithe
   b. bumptious
   c. overweening
   d. petulant

For the following questions, choose the person who would most likely have the characteristic or attitude noted in italics.

51. *blithe*
   a. a soldier in combat
   b. a young child in a playground
   c. the mother of a very sick child
   d. a surgeon during an operation

52. *petulant*
   a. someone who throws a tantrum because his or her soup was not warm enough
   b. someone who is going on an important job interview
   c. someone who needs to earn a little extra money
   d. someone who doesn't like being with other people

53. *puerile*
    a. an infant
    b. a ten year old who has never been given responsibility
    c. a thirty-four year old with too much responsibility
    d. an elderly woman

54. *irascible*
    a. someone who just found out he has a rare disease
    b. someone who just inherited a farm with 200 acres
    c. someone who has just bumped into an old acquaintance, whom she would rather not have seen, from high school
    d. someone waiting for his airplane to take off, only to be told four hours later that his flight has been canceled and his luggage has been lost

55. *saturnine*
    a. someone who just won the lottery
    b. someone who has just fallen in love
    c. someone who has just had a loved one end a relationship
    d. someone who is sleeping

Match the personality traits and attitudes listed in Column A to the descriptions in Column B.

Column A
At a party, a _____ person would most likely be:

Column B

56. bumptious

57. churlish

58. diffident

59. gregarious

60. pretentious

    a. sitting alone in a corner.
    b. talking comfortably with a large group of people.
    c. trying to impress others by telling them everything he or she knows about any given subject.
    d. making ill-mannered and rude remarks.
    e. talking condescendingly to others.

Answers

41. **b.** *Personable* means pleasing in appearance or manner; this is a desirable quality in a roommate.

42. **d.** *Surly* means bad-tempered or unfriendly in a way that suggests menace; this is a very undesirable quality in a roommate.

43. **d.** A *punctilious* person is conscientious and precise, and pays great attention to details, especially in matters of etiquette.

44. **c.** A *perfidious* person is treacherous and dishonest.

45. **b.** A *sagacious* person shows good judgment and is wise.

46. **b.** A *circumspect* person is cautious and watchful.

47. **d.** A *sanguine* person is cheerful and optimistic.

48. **a.** *Craven* means cowardly.

49. **a.** *Capricious* means impulsive and unpredictable; a judge should be consistent in interpreting and applying the law.

50. **c.** An *overweening* supervisor would be presumptuously arrogant and overbearing.

51. **b.** *Blithe* means light-hearted and carefree. Only a young child in a playground is likely to be blithe.

52. **a.** Someone who throws a tantrum because his or her soup was not warm enough is likely to be *petulant*; unreasonably or easily irritated.

53. **b.** A ten year old who has never been given responsibility is likely to be *puerile*; childish and immature.

54. **d.** Someone who has been waiting hours for a flight that is eventually canceled and whose luggage is lost is likely to be *irascible*; irritable and hot-tempered.

55. **c.** *Saturnine* means gloomy and sullen. Choice **c** is the only choice that presents circumstances that would cause someone to be gloomy.

56. **e.** A *bumptious* person would most likely be talking condescendingly to others.

57. **d.** A *churlish* person would make ill-mannered and rude remarks.

58. **a.** A *diffident* person would be shy and would most likely be sitting alone in a corner.

59. **b.** A *gregarious* person would be seeking and enjoying the company of others, and would most likely be talking comfortably with a large group of people.

60. **c.** A *pretentious* person would be showy and would most likely be trying to impress others by telling them everything he or she knows about any given subject.

4

One-Syllable Wonder Words

Have you ever aroused someone's *ire* or enjoyed a day full of *mirth*? These 20 one-syllable wonders prove that words don't have to be long to be interesting or powerful.

Word List

bane (bayn) *n.* 1. cause of trouble, misery, distress, or harm. 2. poison. *The bane of the oak tree is the Asian beetle.*

blight (blīt) *n.* 1. a plant disease that causes the affected parts to wilt and die. 2. something that causes this condition, such as air pollution. 3. something that impairs or destroys. 4. an unsightly object or area. *They still do not know what caused the blight that destroyed half of the trees in the orchard.*

broach (brohch) *v.* 1. to bring up, introduce, in order to begin a discussion of. 2. to tap or pierce, as in to draw off liquid. *It was hard for Sarah to broach the subject of her mother's weight gain.*

cadge (kaj) *v.* to beg, to obtain by begging. *Their dog Cleo would cadge at my feet, hoping I would throw him some table scraps.*

caste (kast) *n.* a distinct social class or system. *While visiting India, Michael was fascinated to learn the particulars of each caste and the way they related to each other.*

daunt (dawnt) *v.* to intimidate, to make afraid or discourage. *Members of the opposing team were trying to daunt the home team by yelling loudly and beating their chests.*

deign (dayn) *v.* to condescend; to unwillingly do something thought to be beneath one's dignity; to lower oneself. *Salvatore deigned to accept money from his father to pay his rent; he had been unemployed for two months.*

dross (draws) *n.* 1. waste product, sludge. 2. something worthless, commonplace, or trivial. *Work crews immediately began the task of cleaning the dross at the abandoned plastics factory.*

eke (eek) *v.* to get or supplement with great effort or strain; to earn or accomplish laboriously. *Working two jobs enabled Quincy to eke out a living wage for his family.*

feign (fayn) *v.* to pretend; to give the false appearance of. *Walter feigned illness to avoid attending the meeting.*

flout (flowt) *v.* to disobey openly and scornfully; to reject, mock, go against (as in a tradition or convention). *Flappers in the early twentieth century would flout convention by bobbing their hair and wearing short skirts.*

guile (gīl) *n.* treacherous cunning; shrewd, crafty deceit. *The most infamous pirates displayed tremendous guile.*

ire (īr) *n.* anger, wrath. *I was filled with ire when Vladimir tried to take credit for my work.*

mete (meet) *v.* to distribute, allot, apportion. *The punishments were meted out fairly to everyone involved in the plot.*

mirth (murth) *n.* great merriment, joyous laughter. *The joyous wedding celebration filled the reception hall with mirth throughout the evening.*

moot (moot) *adj.* debatable, undecided. *The students continued to discuss the moot point, even after class was over.*

pith (pith) *n.* 1. the essential or central part; the heart or essence (of the matter, idea, experience, etc.). 2. (in biology) the soft, sponge-like central cylinder of the stems of most flowering plants. *Her brief, but concise, statement went right to the pith of the argument and covered the most important issues.*

quail (kwayl) *v.* to draw back in fear; flinch, cower. *Mona quailed as soon as Otto, the class bully, entered the room.*

roil (roil) *v.* 1. to make a liquid cloudy or muddy. 2. to stir up or agitate. 3. to anger or annoy. *How could you even think such a thing roils me?*

teem (teem) *v.* to be full of; to be present in large numbers. *The city is teeming with tourists this summer.*

Read sentences 61–70 carefully. Choose a word from the list below that best fills the blank in each sentence.

Word List

bane	daunt
blight	feign
broach	pith
cadge	roil
caste	teem

61. Jane was terribly bored, but she _____(ed) interest so as not to hurt her friend's feelings.

62. At first I felt _____(ed) by the assignment, but then I realized that the problem wasn't as complex as it first seemed.

63. Young Carl's obsession with fire was a _____ for the whole neighborhood.

64. The _____ of my argument is that all life is sacred.

65. He thinks that if he just _____(s) enough, she'll agree to a date.

66. The abandoned building is the only _____ in an otherwise beautiful neighborhood.

67. Their society divides people into several different _____(s) based on their lineage and economic status.

68. The fish tank was _____(ing) with tadpoles.

69. She didn't know how to _____ such a sensitive topic.

70. He is planning a speech that should really _____ the crowd.

Choose the word from the list below that best matches the situation described in each question.

deign	ire
dross	mete
eke	mirth
flout	moot
guile	quail

_____ **71.** students purposely coming to class in clothes forbidden by the dress code

_____ **72.** a corporate spy infiltrating another company to steal proprietary secrets

_____ **73.** what Wanda felt when a competitor opened up a store right across the street from her shop

_____ **74.** something bound to be plentiful in a comedy club

_____ **75.** to make a living in a sweatshop, for example

_____ **76.** a renowned, arrogant singer grudgingly agreeing to tutor a student who lacks talent

_____ **77.** what you might do if you saw a ghost

_____ **78.** what might pollute a river near an industrial site

_____ **79.** giving out rations of food and water at an emergency shelter

_____ **80.** whether or not we should encourage research into the cloning of human beings

Answers

61. To *feign* is to pretend or give a false appearance.

62. To be *daunted* is to be intimidated or discouraged.

63. A *bane* is a cause of trouble, misery, or harm.

64. The *pith* is the essential part or essence (of an idea, argument, etc.).

65. To *cadge* is to beg or obtain by begging.

66. *Blight*, in this context, means an unsightly object or area.

67. A *caste* is a distinct social class, system, or group.

68. To *teem* is to be full of or present in large numbers.

69. To *broach* is to bring up or introduce in order to begin a discussion of a topic or issue.

70. To *roil* in this context means to stir up or agitate; to anger or annoy. *Roil* can also mean to make (a liquid) cloudy or muddy.

71. To *flout* is to disobey openly or scornfully; to reject, mock, or go against (a tradition or convention).

72. *Guile* means treacherous cunning or shrewd; crafty deceit.

73. *Ire* means anger or wrath.

74. *Mirth* means great merriment or joyous laughter.

75. To *eke* is to get with great effort or strain; to earn or accomplish laboriously.

76. To *deign* is to condescend; to do something thought to be beneath one's dignity.

77. To *quail* is to draw back in fear; to cower.

78. *Dross* means waste product or sludge. It can also mean something worthless, commonplace, or trivial.

79. To *mete* is to distribute, allot, or apportion.

80. A *moot* issue is something that is debatable or undecided. *Note:* The phrase *moot point* has come to mean a point not worth discussing because it has no value or relevance. This is a non-standard use of the word, but one that has come to be accepted. Be sure your meaning is clear when you use this word.

5

Lights, Camera, Action—Vivid Verbs

Have you ever been *upbraided* or *stultified*? The 20 verbs in this chapter describe actions that are powerful or invoke vivid images.

Word List

abrogate ('ab·rŏ·gayt) *v.* to abolish, do away with, or annul by authority. *It was unclear if the judge would abrogate the lower court's ruling.*

beguile (bi·'gīl) *v.* to deceive or cheat through cunning; to distract the attention of, divert; to pass time in a pleasant manner, to amuse or charm. *Violet was able to beguile the spy, causing him to miss his secret meeting.*

bolster ('bohl·stĕr) *v.* 1. to support or prop up. 2. to buoy or hearten. *Coach Edmond's speech bolstered the team's confidence.*

burgeon ('bur·jŏn) *v.* to begin to grow and flourish; to begin to sprout, grow new buds, blossom. *The tulip bulbs beneath the soil would burgeon in early spring, providing there was no late frost.*

burnish ('bur·nish) *v.* to polish, rub to a shine. *When Kathryn began to burnish the old metal teapot, she realized that it was, in fact, solid silver.*

careen (kă·'reen) *v.* 1. to lurch from side to side while in motion. 2. to rush carelessly or headlong. *Watching the car in front of us careen down the road was very frightening.*

decimate ('des·ĭ·mayt) *v.* to destroy a large portion of. *An extended period of neglect would eventually decimate much of the housing in the inner cities.*

deprecate ('dep·rĕ·kayt) *v.* to express disapproval of; to belittle, depreciate. *Grandpa's tendency to deprecate the children's friends was a frequent source of family strife.*

fetter ('fet·ĕr) *v.* 1. to shackle, put in chains. 2. to impede or restrict. *The presence of two security guards fettered the teenagers' plans to get backstage.*

forestall (fohr·'stawl) *v.* to prevent by taking action first; preempt. *The diplomat was able to forestall a conflict by holding secret meetings with both parties.*

fulminate ('ful·mĭ·nayt) *v.* 1. to issue a thunderous verbal attack; berate. 2. to explode or detonate. *The senator was prone to fulminate when other legislators questioned her ideology.*

immolate ('im·ŏ·layt) *v.* 1. to kill, as a sacrifice. 2. to ruin by fire. 3. to destroy (one thing for another). *In a desperate attempt to make a point about what she considered an inappropriate book, Sophia decided to immolate the book in public.*

interdict (in·tĕr·'dikt) *v.* to prohibit, forbid. *Carlos argued that the agriculture department should interdict plans to produce genetically modified foods.*

inveigle (in·ˈvay·gĕl) *v.* to influence or persuade through gentle coaxing or flattery; to entice. *Vanessa inveigled her way into a promotion that should have gone to Maxon.*

petrify (ˈpet·rĭ·fī) *v.* 1. to make hard or stiff like a stone. 2. to stun or paralyze with fear, astonishment, or dread. *I was petrified when I heard the door open in the middle of the night.*

pique (peek) *v.* to wound (someone's) pride, to offend; to arouse or provoke. *The article really piqued my interest in wildlife preservation.*

stultify (ˈstul·tĭ·fī) *v.* 1. to impair or make ineffective; to cripple. 2. to make (someone) look foolish or incompetent. *Of course I'm angry! You stultified me at that meeting!*

subvert (sub·ˈvurt) *v.* 1. to overthrow. 2. to ruin, destroy completely. 3. to undermine. *She quietly subverted his authority by sharing internal information with outside agents.*

truncate (ˈtrung·kayt) *v.* to shorten or terminate by (or as if by) cutting the top or end off. *The glitch in the software program truncated the lines of a very important document I was typing.*

upbraid (up·ˈbrayd) *v.* to reprove, reproach sharply, condemn; admonish. *The child was upbraided for misbehaving during the ceremony.*

Match the person or thing in Column A with the action he, she, or it might perform in Column B.

Column A	Column B
81. slaveholder, to a slave	beguile
82. a rosebush in spring	burgeon
83. a lawmaking authority, to its constituents	careen
84. a tornado or earthquake, to a city	decimate
85. a car out of control	fetter
86. a mother, to a misbehaving child	fulminate
87. a ghost in a horror movie	interdict
88. a desperate political candidate, against his opponent	petrify
89. a small-time swindler	subvert
90. a group of rebels, to a government	upbraid

Read sentences 91–100 carefully. Choose the verb from the list below that best completes each sentence.

abrogate	immolate
bolster	inveigle
burnish	pique
deprecate	stultify
forestall	truncated

91. I can't believe Charlie would try to _____ me in front of my boss like that!

92. He thinks he can just _____ everyone he meets, but not everyone falls for that kind of flattery.

93. His flagging spirits were _____(ed) by the news that a publisher had accepted his manuscript.

94. Once a month, I spend a Saturday afternoon _____(ing) my silverware.

95. Saul _____(ed) every remark that Bernadette made, and she grew weary of his interruptions.

96. Her career as a dancer was _____(ed) because of a skiing accident.

97. The strike was _____(ed) by last-minute concessions by management.

98. At the end of *Frankenstein*, the creature _____(s) himself in a giant funeral pyre.

99. The new president rashly _____(ed) all of the laws passed by his predecessor.

100. Listening to the lecture has really _____(ed) my interest in science fiction.

Answers

81. To *fetter* is to shackle or put in chains. It can also mean to impede or restrict.

82. To *burgeon* is to begin to grow and flourish; to begin to sprout, grow new buds, blossom.

83. To *interdict* means to prohibit or forbid.

84. To *decimate* something is to destroy a large portion of it.

85. To *careen* is to lurch from side to side while in motion or to rush carelessly or headlong.

86. To *upbraid* is to reprove or reproach sharply; to admonish or condemn.

87. To *petrify* in this context is to stun or paralyze with fear, astonishment, or dread. *Petrify* can also mean to make hard or stiff like a stone.

88. To *fulminate* is to issue a thunderous verbal attack, to berate. It can also mean to explode or detonate.

89. To *beguile* is to deceive or cheat through cunning. It can also mean to distract the attention of or to pass time in a pleasant manner.

90. To *subvert* means to overthrow, to ruin completely, or to undermine.

91. To *stultify* in this context means to make someone look foolish or incompetent. It can also mean to impair or make ineffective; to cripple.

92. To *inveigle* means to influence or persuade through gentle coaxing or flattery; to entice.

93. To *bolster* means to buoy or hearten. It can also mean to support or prop up.

94. To *burnish* is to polish; to rub to a shine.

95. To *deprecate* is to express disapproval of; to belittle.

96. To *truncate* is to shorten or terminate by (or as if by) cutting the top or end off.

97. To *forestall* is to preempt; to prevent by taking action first.

98. To *immolate* is to kill oneself by fire. It can also mean to kill as a sacrifice or to destroy (one thing for another).

99. To *abrogate* is to abolish or annul by authority.

100. To *pique* is to arouse or provoke; it can also mean to wound someone's pride or offend.

6

Crime and Punishment

Have you ever been guilty of a *peccadillo* or been *exculpated* for something you didn't do? These 20 words are all associated with crimes and their punishments.

Word List

abscond (ab·ˈskond) *v.* to run away secretly and hide, often in order to avoid arrest or prosecution. *Criminals will often head south and abscond with stolen goods to Mexico.*

absolution (ab·sŏ·ˈloo·shŏn) *n.* 1. an absolving or clearing from blame or guilt. 2. a formal declaration of forgiveness; redemption. *The jury granted Anna the absolution she deserved.*

bilk (bilk) *v.* to deceive or defraud; to swindle or cheat, especially to evade paying one's debts. *The stockbroker was led away in handcuffs, accused of trying to bilk senior citizens out of their investment dollars.*

castigate (ˈkas·tĭ·gayt) *v.* to inflict a severe punishment on; to chastise severely. *When she was caught stealing for the second time, Maya knew her mother would castigate her.*

chastise (chas·ˈtīz) *v.* to punish severely; to criticize harshly, rebuke. *Charles knew that his wife would chastise him after he inadvertently told the room full of guests that she had just had a face-lift.*

collusion (kŏ·ˈloo·zhŏn) *n.* a secret agreement between two or more people for a deceitful or fraudulent purpose; conspiracy. *The discovery of the e-mail proved that collusion existed between the CEO and CFO to defraud the shareholders.*

enormity (i·ˈnor·mi·tee) *n.* 1. excessive wickedness. 2. a monstrous offense or evil act; atrocity. *The enormity of Jeffrey Dahmer's crimes will never be forgotten.*
Note: Enormity is often used to indicate something of great size (e.g., the enormity of the task), but this is considered an incorrect use of the word.

exculpate (eks·ˈkul·payt) *v.* to free from blame, to clear from a charge of guilt. *When Anthony admitted to committing the crime, it served to exculpate Marcus.*

malfeasance (măl·ˈfee·zăns) *n.* misconduct or wrongdoing, especially by a public official; improper professional conduct. *The city comptroller was found guilty of malfeasance and removed from office.*

miscreant (ˈmis·kree·ănt) *n.* a villain, criminal; evil person. *The miscreant had eluded the police for months, but today he was finally captured.*

peccadillo (pek·ă·ˈdil·oh) *n.* a trivial offense; a small sin or fault. *Don't make such a big deal out of a little peccadillo.*

perjury ('pur·jŭ·ree) *n.* the deliberate willful giving of false, misleading, or incomplete testimony while under oath. *William was convicted of perjury for lying about his whereabouts on the night of the crime.*

purloin (pŭr·'loin) *v.* to steal. *The thief purloined a sculpture worth thousands of dollars.*

recalcitrant (ri·'kal·si·trănt) *adj.* disobedient, unruly; refusing to obey authority. *The recalcitrant child was sent to the principal's office for the third time in a week.*

recidivism (ri·'sid·ĭ·vizm) *n.* a relapse or backslide, especially into antisocial or criminal behavior after conviction and punishment. *Allowing prisoners to earn their GED or a college degree has been shown to greatly reduce recidivism.*

reprehensible (rep·ri·'hen·sĭ·běl) *adj.* deserving rebuke or censure. *The reprehensible behavior of the neighborhood bully angered everyone on the block.*

reprieve (ri·'preev) *n.* 1. postponement or cancellation of punishment, especially of the death sentence. 2. temporary relief from danger or discomfort. *The court granted him a reprieve at the last moment because of DNA evidence that absolved him.*

tribunal (trī·'byoo·năl) *n.* a court of justice. *He will be sentenced for his war crimes by an international tribunal.*

turpitude ('tur·pi·tood) *n.* 1. wickedness. 2. a corrupt or depraved act. *Such turpitude deserves the most severe punishment.*

venal ('vee·năl) *adj.* easily bribed or corrupted; unprincipled. *The venal judge was removed and disbarred.*

Match the action described in Column A with the name of the crime or criminal nature in Column B.

Column A

101. lying under oath

102. conspiring to rig a local election

103. a politician using public funds to buy gifts for his or her family

104. telling a white lie

105. committing armed robbery after serving time for auto theft

106. a defendant trying to leave the state before his or her case goes to trial: attempting to _____

107. frequently accepting bribes while in office: a _____ public official

108. taking something that belongs to someone else

109. swindling a rich divorcee: _____(ing) an innocent woman

110. executing the entire population of a village during a civil war

Column B

abscond

bilk

collusion

enormity

malfeasance

peccadillo

perjury

purloin

recidivism

venal

Using the words from the list below, choose the best word to complete each of the following sentences.

absolution   recalcitrant

castigate   reprehensible

chastise   reprieve

exculpate   tribunal

miscreant   turpitude

111. The international _____ will hear more testimony today regarding the general's wartime atrocities.

112. The evidence was sufficient to _____ her from the crime.

113. The new district attorney refused to condone the mayor's _____ behavior.

114. Catholics believe that going to confession gives them _____ from their sins.

115. The Athenian lawmaker Draco was known to _____ citizens for the most minor offenses.

116. The _____ students were given two-week suspensions and required to complete 20 hours of community service.

117. Edna _____ (ed) the children for not doing their homework.

118. The _____ of the crime shocked even the most hardened detectives.

119. The judge granted Mason a _____ when another man confessed to the crime.

120. The worst _____ (s) are often those who appear to lead normal, law-abiding lives.

Answers

101. To commit *perjury* is to deliberately give false, misleading, or incomplete testimony while under oath.

102. *Collusion* is a conspiracy; a secret agreement between two or more people for a fraudulent purpose.

103. *Malfeasance* is misconduct or wrongdoing, especially by a public official.

104. A *peccadillo* is a small sin or fault; a trivial offense.

105. *Recidivism* means a relapse or backslide into criminal behavior after conviction and punishment.

106. To *abscond* is to run away secretly and hide, usually in order to avoid arrest or prosecution.

107. *Venal* means easily bribed or corrupted; unprincipled.

108. To *purloin* means to steal.

109. To *bilk* means to deceive or defraud; to swindle or cheat, especially to evade paying one's debts.

110. *Enormity* means excessive wickedness or a monstrous offense or evil act; an atrocity.

111. A *tribunal* is a court of justice.

112. To *exculpate* means to free from blame or clear from a charge of guilt.

113. *Reprehensible* means deserving rebuke or censure; deserving of strong criticism or disapproval.

114. *Absolution* is an absolving or clearing from blame or guilt; a formal declaration of forgiveness or redemption.

115. To *castigate* means to inflict a severe punishment on; to chastise severely. *Castigate* implies a harsher punishment than *chastise*, which also means to punish severely but can also mean to criticize harshly. *Castigate* is therefore more appropriate in the context of this sentence.

116. *Recalcitrant* means disobedient; unruly, refusing to obey authority.

117. To *chastise* means to punish severely or to criticize harshly. Here, the context suggests harsh criticism rather than severe punishment.

118. *Turpitude* means wickedness. It also means a corrupt or depraved act.

119. A *reprieve* is a postponement or cancellation of punishment, especially of the death sentence. It can also mean temporary relief from danger or discomfort.

120. A *miscreant* is a villain, criminal, or evil person.

7

To Be or Not To Be

Have you ever been offended by a *boor* or charmed by someone with a very *genteel* nature? The 20 words in this chapter describe many different kinds of people—some you might like to have as family and friends, and many you would not. You can find the answers to each question in this section at the end of the chapter.

Word List

boor (boor) *n.* a crude, offensive, ill-mannered person. *Seeing Chuck wipe his mouth with his sleeve, Maribel realized she was attending her senior prom with a classic boor.*

bourgeois (boor·ʹzhwah) *adj.* typical of the middle class; conforming to the standards and conventions of the middle class. *A house in the suburbs, two children, two cars, and three TVs are key indicators of a bourgeois lifestyle.*

chauvinist (ʹshoh·vĭn·ist) *n.* a person who believes in the superiority of his or her own kind; an extreme nationalist. *Male chauvinists believe that women are mentally and physically inferior to men.*

erudite (ʹer·yŭ·dīt) *adj.* having or showing great learning; profoundly educated, scholarly. *The scholarly work of nonfiction was obviously written by an erudite young student.*

fatuous (ʹfach·oo·ŭs) *adj.* complacently stupid; feeble-minded and silly. *Since Sam was such an intellectually accomplished student, Mr. Britt was surprised to discover that Sam's well-meaning but fatuous parents were not at all like him.*

feckless (ʹfek·lis) *adj.* 1. lacking purpose or vitality; feeble, weak. 2. incompetent and ineffective, careless. *Jake's feckless performance led to his termination from the team.*

genteel (jen·ʹteel) *adj.* elegantly polite, well-bred; refined. *The genteel host made sure that each entrée was cooked to each guest's specifications.*

iconoclast (ī·ʹkon·oh·klast) *n.* 1. a person who attacks and seeks to overthrow traditional ideas, beliefs, or institutions. 2. someone who opposes and destroys idols used in worship. *Using words as weapons, the well-spoken iconoclast challenged religious hypocrisy wherever she found it.*

ignoble (ig·ʹnoh·bĕl) *adj.* 1. lacking nobility in character or purpose; dishonorable. 2. not of the nobility, common. *Mark was an ignoble successor to such a well-respected leader, so many members of the organization resigned.*

libertine (ʹlib·ĕr·teen) *n.* one who lives or acts in an immoral or irresponsible way; one who acts according to his or her own impulses and desires; unrestrained by conventions or morals. *They claim to be avant-garde, but in my opinion, they're just a bunch of libertines.*

maladroit (mal·ă·ʹdroit) *adj.* clumsy, bungling; inept. *The maladroit waiter broke a dozen plates and spilled coffee on two customers.*

maverick ('mav·ĕr·ik) *n.* rebel, nonconformist; one who acts independently. *Madonna has always been a maverick in the music industry.*

obtuse (ŏb·'toos) *adj.* 1. stupid and slow to understand. 2. blunt, not sharp or pointed. *Please don't be so obtuse; you know what I mean.*

philistine ('fil·i·steen) *n.* a smug, ignorant person; someone who is uncultured and commonplace. *Richards thinks he is cosmopolitan, but he's really just a philistine.*

poseur (poh·'zur) *n.* someone who puts on airs to impress others; a phony. *My first impression of the arrogant newcomer was that he was a poseur; I just had a hunch that he wasn't what he seemed to be.*

renegade ('ren·ĕ·gayd) *n.* 1. a deserter; one who rejects a cause, group, etc. 2. a person who rebels and becomes an outlaw. *The renegade soldier decided to join the guerilla fighters.*

reprobate ('rep·rŏ·bayt) *n.* an immoral or unprincipled person; one without scruples. *Edgar deemed himself a reprobate, a criminal, and a traitor in his written confession.*

rogue (rohg) *n.* 1. a dishonest, unprincipled person. 2. a pleasantly mischievous person. 3. a vicious and solitary animal living apart from the herd. *Yesterday, that rogue hid all of my cooking utensils; today he's switched everything around in the cupboards!*

sycophant ('sik·ŏ·fănt) *n.* a person who tries to win the favor of influential or powerful people through flattery; a fawning parasite. *The president is surrounded by sycophants, so how will he really know if his ideas have merit?*

urbane (ur·'bayn) *adj.* elegant, highly refined in manners; extremely tactful and polite. *Christopher thinks he's so urbane, but he's really quite pedestrian.*

For numbers 121–130, read the following sentences carefully. Decide which answer best describes the italicized vocabulary word and circle the letter of the correct answer. If you do not own this book, please write your answers on a separate piece of paper.

121. A *boor* would be likely to
   a. interrupt everyone's conversation at the dinner table.
   b. be a gracious host or hostess.
   c. be the life of the party.
   d. be quiet and reserved.

122. If you had a *rogue* for a roommate, you might expect him to
   a. work diligently to keep his grades up.
   b. keep his room sparkling clean.
   b. steal your homework and turn it in as his own.
   b. be very religious.

123. A *renegade* soldier would likely
   a. be recognized for bravery.
   b. suffer from debilitating injuries.
   c. desert his unit.
   d. be admired by his fellow soldiers.

124. If you were a *libertine*, you might
   a. become a freedom fighter defending the principles of democracy.
   b. intentionally drive the wrong way down a one-way street.
   c. adhere to the rules and laws governing the liberty you enjoy.
   d. not drink anything containing alcohol.

125. If your English professor was very *erudite*, she would be
   a. scholarly and highly educated.
   b. a little absentminded.
   c. very young and inexperienced.
   d. very elderly and set in her ways.

126. A *feckless* teammate would likely
   a. come in first place in most races.
   b. attend every practice.
   c. show no enthusiasm for the sport or competition.
   d. be the team captain.

127. A *maladroit* juggler would likely
    a. be able to juggle ten or more balls at a time.
    b. drop the balls as frequently as he caught them.
    c. be a beginning juggler.
    d. juggle very heavy objects.

128. If you were *urbane*, you would
    a. have highly refined manners and etiquette.
    b. live in a city or urban area.
    c. be caustic and unpleasant.
    d. have a false pretense.

129. If your banker were a *reprobate*, he or she would likely
    a. ensure that your money was turned over to your heirs in the event of your death.
    b. make careful documentation of every transaction and payment.
    c. misappropriate funds.
    d. have a sloppy, unprofessional appearance.

130. If a family were described as being *bourgeois*, you would probably find them
    a. living in France.
    b. living in poverty.
    c. living a middle-class lifestyle.
    d. living a wealthy lifestyle.

For numbers 131–140, read the following sentences carefully. Decide which vocabulary word best matches the character described in the sentence and circle the letter of the correct answer. If you do not own this book, please write your answers on a separate piece of paper.

131. If you are someone who puts on airs to impress others, you are a(n)
   a. philistine.
   b. poseur.
   c. boor.
   d. iconoclast.

132. A film director who defies convention and pursues his or her own vision is a
   a. rogue.
   b. maverick.
   c. sycophant.
   d. chauvinist.

133. Someone who fails to understand simple directions even when they are explained repeatedly would be called
   a. ignoble.
   b. bourgeois.
   c. maladroit.
   d. obtuse.

134. Martin Luther, who during the sixteenth century publicly criticized the practices and leadership of the Roman Catholic Church, would rightfully be called a(n)
   a. ignoble.
   b. iconoclast.
   c. philistine.
   d. chauvinist.

135. If an authority figure was often seen drunk and disorderly, his or her behavior would be referred to as
   a. erudite.
   b. urbane.
   c. genteel.
   d. ignoble.

136. If your roommate has no interest in developing his or her own intelligence, your roommate could be described as
   a. erudite.
   b. urbane.
   c. fatuous.
   d. maladroit.

137. Someone who believes himself to be fabulously cultured and smart but in truth is really very commonplace could be described as a(n)
   a. maverick.
   b. sycophant.
   c. philistine.
   d. iconoclast.

138. A man who opens doors for women and rises from his seat when a woman arrives at or leaves the table would be called
   a. genteel.
   b. urbane.
   c. feckless.
   d. maladroit.

139. A woman who believes that women are superior to men is a(n)
   a. sycophant.
   b. chauvinist.
   c. philistine.
   d. iconoclast.

140. Someone who works for a powerful leader and repeatedly offers the leader praise and flattery even when it is undeserved would be a
   a. sycophant.
   b. chauvinist.
   c. boor.
   d. philistine.

Answers

121. **a.** A *boor* is a crude and offensive person; someone who is ill-mannered.

122. **c.** A *rogue* is a dishonest, unprincipled person.

123. **c.** A *renegade* is one who deserts a group or cause.

124. **b.** A *libertine* is someone who acts in an immoral or irresponsible way.

125. **a.** To be *erudite* is to be scholarly and exceptionally educated.

126. **c.** To be *feckless* is to demonstrate a lack of purpose or vitality.

127. **b.** To be *maladroit* is to be clumsy and inept.

128. **a.** To be *urbane* is to have highly refined manners; extremely tactful and polite.

129. **c.** A *reprobate* is an immoral and unprincipled person.

130. **c.** *Bourgeois* means characterized by or typical of the middle class.

131. **b.** A *poseur* is someone who puts on airs, or is phony in order to impress others.

132. **b.** A *maverick* is a nonconformist, someone who acts independently.

133. **d.** Someone who is *obtuse* is stupid and slow to understand.

134. **b.** An *iconoclast* attacks and may even seek to overthrow traditional ideas, beliefs, or institutions.

135. **d.** Someone who is *ignoble* lacks nobility in their character.

136. **c.** To be *fatuous* is to be complacently stupid.

137. **c.** A *philistine* is a smug, ignorant person who is actually uncultured and commonplace.

138. **a.** To be *genteel* is to be elegantly polite, well-bred, and refined.

139. **b.** A *chauvinist* is a person who believes in the superiority of his or her own gender.

140. **a.** A *sycophant* is a person who tries to win the favor of influential or powerful people by flattering them.

8

Word Pairs II

Do *dulcet* or *mellifluous* sounds please you? Or would you prefer to listen to music that is *banal* or *pedestrian*? This is the second of four chapters of *word pairs*—pairs of words that are almost exactly the same in meaning. Each word pair chapter contains ten sets of synonyms. You can find the answers to each question in this section at the end of the chapter.

Word List

aberration (ăb·ĕ·´ray·shŏn) *n.* deviation from what is normal; distortion. *His new scientific theory was deemed an aberration by his very conservative colleagues.*

abstruse (ab·´stroos) *adj.* difficult to comprehend; obscure. *Albert Einstein's abstruse calculations can be understood by only a few people.*

anomaly (ă·´nom·ă·lee) *n.* something that deviates from the general rule or usual form; irregular, peculiar, or abnormal. *Winning millions of dollars from a slot machine would be considered an anomaly.*

assiduous (ă·´sij·oo·ŭs) *adj.* diligent, persevering, unremitting; constant in application or attention. *The nurses in the intensive care unit are known for providing assiduous care to their patients.*

august (aw·´gust) *adj.* majestic, venerable; inspiring admiration or reverence. *Jackie Kennedy's august dignity in the days following her husband's assassination set a tone for the rest of the nation as it mourned.*

banal (bā·´nal) *adj.* commonplace, trite; obvious and uninteresting. *Though Tom and Susan had hoped for an adventure, they found that driving cross-country on the interstate offered mostly banal sites, restaurants, and attractions.*

boisterous (´boi·stĕ·rŭs) *adj.* 1. loud, noisy, and lacking restraint or discipline. 2. stormy and rough. *The boisterous crowd began throwing cups onto the field during the football game.*

dulcet (´dul·sit) *adj.* melodious, harmonious, sweet-sounding. *The chamber orchestra's dulcet tunes were a perfect ending to a great evening.*

epitome (i·´pit·ŏ·mee) *n.* 1. something or someone that embodies a particular quality or characteristic; a representative example or a typical model. 2. a brief summary or abstract. *With his ten-gallon hat, western shirt, and rugged jeans, Alex was the epitome of the American cowboy.*

impudent (´im·pyŭ·dĕnt) *adj.* 1. boldly showing a lack of respect, insolent. 2. shamelessly forward, immodest. *Thumbing his nose at the principal was an impudent act.*

insolent (´in·sŏ·lĕnt) *adj.* haughty and contemptuous; brazen, disrespectful, impertinent. *Parents of teenagers often observe the insolent behavior that typically accompanies adolescence.*

mellifluous (me·´lif·loo·ŭs) *adj.* sounding sweet and flowing; honeyed. *Her mellifluous voice floated in through the windows and made everyone smile.*

ostensible (o·'sten·sĭ·bĕl) *adj.* seeming, appearing as such, put forward (as of a reason) but not necessarily so; pretended. *The ostensible reason for the meeting is to discuss the candidates, but I believe they have already made their decision.*

pedestrian (pĕ·'des·tri·ăn) *adj.* commonplace, trite; unremarkable, unimaginative; dull. *Although the film received critical acclaim, its pedestrian plot has been overused by screenwriters for decades.*

purport ('pur·pohrt) *v.* 1. to be intended to seem, to have the appearance of being. 2. propose or intend. *The letter purports to express your opinion on the matter.*

quintessence (kwin·'tes·ĕns) *n.* 1. the essence of a substance. 2. the perfect example or embodiment of something. *Maura is the quintessence of kindness.*

raucous ('raw·'kŭs) *adj.* 1. unpleasantly loud and harsh. 2. boisterous, disorderly; disturbing the peace. *The raucous music kept us awake all night.*

recondite ('rek·ŏn·dīt) *adj.* 1. not easily understood; obscure and abstruse. 2. dealing with abstruse or profound matters. *He loves the challenge of grasping a recondite subject.*

sedulous ('sej·ŭ·lŭs) *adj.* diligent, persevering; hardworking. *After years of sedulous research, the researchers discovered a cure.*

venerable ('ven·ĕ·ră·'bĕl) *adj.* worthy of reverence or respect because of age, dignity, character, or position. *The venerable Jimmy Carter has just won the Nobel Peace Prize.*

Crossword Puzzle Directions

In this puzzle, there is one clue for each set of synonyms, so each clue is offered twice. Read the definition provided in the clue and determine which two words share that meaning. Then, determine which of those synonyms fits in the designated crossword squares. (Note: All pairs are the same part of speech except one pair which contains a verb and a noun.)

Word Pairs II Crossword Puzzle

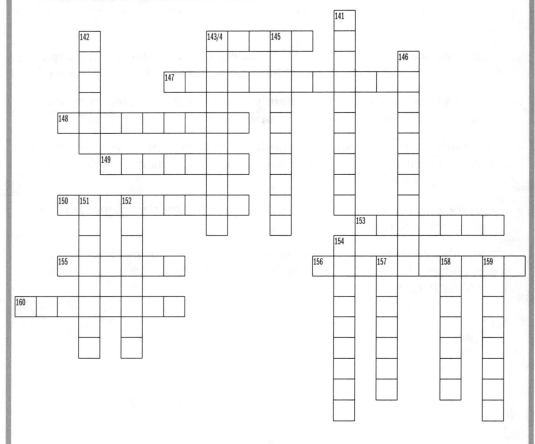

ACROSS

143. commonplace, trite, uninteresting (paired with 156 across)

147. a representative or perfect example (paired with 157 down)

148. not easily understood, obscure (paired with 159 down)

149. to be intended to seem (verb); seeming one way but not necessarily so (adjective) (paired with 141 down)

150. diligent, hard-working, persevering (paired with 151 down)

153. something that deviates from what is normal or standard (paired with 145 down)

155. inspiring admiration or respect; majestic (paired with 154 down)

156. commonplace, trite, uninteresting (paired with 143 across)

160. brazenly disrespectful (paired with 152 down)

DOWN

141. to be intended to seem (verb); seeming one way but not necessarily so (adjective) (paired with 149 across)

142. sweet-sounding, harmonious (paired with 146 down)

144. excessively loud, unrestrained (paired with 158 down)

146. sweet-sounding, harmonious (paired with 142 down)

151. diligent, hard working, persevering (paired with 150 across)

152. brazenly disrespectful (paired with 160 across)

154. inspiring admiration or respect, majestic (paired with 155 across)

157. a representative or perfect example (paired with 147 across)

158. excessively loud, unrestrained (paired with 143 down)

159. not easily understood, obscure (paired with 148 across)

Answers

The following words are *word pairs*:

aberration, anomaly
dulcet, mellifluous
impudent, insolent
august, venerable
assiduous, sedulous
boisterous, raucous
quintessence, epitome
banal, pedestrian
recondite, abstruse
purport, ostensible

Across

143. Something *banal* is very common, uninteresting, and trite; *pedestrian*.

147. *Quintessence* is the essence of something; a perfect example or embodiment; *epitome*.

148. If something is *recondite*, it is difficult to understand; obscure and *abstruse*.

149. To *purport* is to be intended to seem, to have the appearance of being; to be *ostensible*. (*Purport* is a verb; *ostensible* is an adjective.)

150. To do something in an *assiduous* manner is to be diligent and unremitting; *sedulous*.

153. An *anomaly* is something that is irregular, a deviation from the norm; an *aberration*.

155. To be *august* is to inspire reverence or admiration; *venerable*.

156. Something *pedestrian* is commonplace, unimaginative, or dull; *banal*.

160. To be *insolent* is to be brazenly disrespectful; contemptuous, *impudent*.

Down

141. Something *ostensible* seems one way but is not necessarily so; pretended or *purported*. (*Ostensible* is an adjective; *purport* is a verb, with *purported* as its adjective form.)

142. *Dulcet* means very sweet, especially sweet sounding; *mellifluous*.

144. To be *boisterous* is to be unpleasantly loud and unrestrained; *raucous*.

145. An *aberration* is a deviation from the norm, an *anomaly*.

146. To be *mellifluous* is to be sweet-sounding and flowing; *dulcet*.

151. To be *sedulous* is to be diligent and hardworking; *assiduous*.

152. To be *impudent* is to boldly show a lack of respect; to be *insolent*.

154. To be *venerable* is to be worthy of admiration or respect; *august*.

157. An *epitome* is a perfect example of something; *quintessence*.

158. To be *raucous* is to be unpleasantly loud and harsh; *boisterous*.

159. Something *abstruse* is difficult to understand; obscure, *recondite*.

9

What's It Like? Appearances and Conditions

Have you ever been bored by a *mundane* task or looked over the edge of a *precipitous* cliff? The 20 vocabulary words in this chapter offer more precise and elegant descriptions of conditions and appearances. You can find the answers to each question in this section at the end of the chapter.

Word List

abysmal (ă·ˈbiz·măl) *adj.* 1. extreme, very profound, limitless. 2. extremely bad. *Tom's last place finish in the race was an abysmal turn of events for the team.*

ad hoc (ad ˈhok) *adj.* for a specific, often temporary, purpose; for this case only. *She acted as the ad hoc scout leader while Mr. Davis—the official leader—was ill.*

amorphous (ă·ˈmor·fŭs) *adj.* having no definite shape or form; shapeless. *The amorphous cloud of steam drifted over her head.*

askew (ă·ˈskyoo) *adj. & adv.* crooked, not straight or level; to one side. *Even the pictures on the wall stood askew after my five-year-old son's birthday party.*

fecund (ˈfek·ŭnd) *adj.* fertile. *The fecund soil in the valley was able to sustain the growing community.*

flaccid (ˈfla·sid) *adj.* hanging loose or wrinkled; weak, flabby, not firm. *The skin of cadavers becomes flaccid in a matter of hours.*

florid (ˈflor·id) *adj.* 1. elaborate, ornate. 2. (of complexion) ruddy, rosy. *The florid architecture in Venice does not appeal to me; I prefer buildings without so much ornamentation.*

hermetic (hur·ˈmet·ik) *adj.* having an airtight closure; protected from outside influences. *Astronauts go for space walks only when wearing hermetic space suits.*

malleable (ˈmal·i·ă·bĕl) *adj.* 1. easily molded or pressed into shape. 2. easily controlled or influenced. 3. easily adaptable to changing circumstances. *You should be able to convince Xiu quickly; she's quite a malleable person.*

mundane (mun·ˈdayn) *adj.* 1. dull, routine; commonplace, ordinary. 2. worldly as opposed to spiritual. *My job may be mundane, but it is secure and it pays well.*

precarious (pri·ˈkair·i·ŭs) *adj.* 1. fraught with danger. 2. dangerously unsteady or insecure. *Steve, the "Crocodile Hunter," is constantly placing himself in very precarious positions.*

precipitous (pri·ˈsip·i·tŭs) *adj.* 1. extremely steep, dropping sharply. 2. hasty, rash; foolhardy. *Driving through the state park, we spotted a grizzly bear on a precipitous cliff and wondered if he would fall.*

pristine (ˈpris·teen) *adj.* 1. in its original and unspoiled condition, unadulterated. 2. clean, pure; free from contamination. *We were awed by the beauty of the pristine forest in northern Canada.*

quiescent (kwi·ˈes·ĕnt) *adj.* inactive, quiet, at rest; dormant, latent. *The volcano is quiescent at the moment, but who knows when it will erupt again.*

rakish (ˈray·kish) *adj.* 1. debonair; smartly dressed or mannered; jaunty in appearance or manner. 2. unconventional and disreputable; dissolute or debauched. *The rakish young woman charmed everyone at the table.*

replete (ri·ˈpleet) *adj.* 1. well-stocked or abundantly supplied. 2. full, gorged. *The house was replete with expensive antiques.*

salutary (ˈsal·yŭ·ter·ee) *adj.* producing a beneficial or wholesome effect; remedial. *To promote better health, I've decided to move to a more salutary climate.*

sinuous (ˈsin·yoo·ŭs) *adj.* winding, undulating; serpentine. *It is dangerous to drive fast on such a sinuous road.*

sodden (ˈsod·ĕn) *adj.* 1. thoroughly saturated, soaked. 2. expressionless or dull, unimaginative. *Caught in an unexpected rainstorm, I was sodden by the time I reached the bus stop.*

tenuous (ˈten·yoo·ŭs) *adj.* 1. unsubstantial, flimsy. 2. having little substance or validity. *Though the connection between the two crimes seemed tenuous at first, a thorough investigation showed they were committed by the same person.*

For numbers 161–180, choose the vocabulary word that best fills the blank in the sentence. Write the correct answer in the blank. (If you do not own this book, please write your answers on a separate piece of paper.)

161. The dry modeling clay was no longer _____ after the young boys left it uncovered overnight.

162. The tutoring Shelia received had a(n) _____ effect on her grade point average.

163. The _____ ceiling of the palace contained a very colorful and detailed painting that was surrounded by gold leaf moldings.

164. Carl realized he had hit the jackpot when he opened his grandfather's safe deposit box and found a 1921 era baseball card in _____ condition.

165. Running out of gas in the middle of the desert in August was a(n) _____ turn of events.

166. The CIA agent put herself in a very _____ situation by sneaking into the embassy.

167. Being a toll collector on the highway was a very _____ job for Vladimir, an engineer by trade.

168. Because Pasquale had only a(n) _____ understanding of the subject matter, he failed the test.

169. The minor earthquake left everything in my house _____.

170. The movie star's _____ appearance captured the attention of everyone in the room.

171. The dry cleaner said that putting the antique wedding dress in a _____ container would protect it from the elements.

172. Don't expect young children to act in a(n) _____ manner when attending a birthday party; they will be much too excited.

173. The galley of the ship was _____ with food for the long journey.

174. Matthew's sneakers were _____ after jumping in every puddle on the block.

175. The mist rising off the lake was _____ and therefore difficult for the artist to capture on the canvas.

176. "If you want _____ soil," said the farmer, "you must add fertilizer in the spring."

177. When the power went out, Tim acted as a(n) _____ traffic cop until the police arrived.

178. Old-fashioned rollercoasters don't have upside down loops, but they do have very _____ tracks that rock riders back and forth.

179. As a novice mountain climber, Maria wasn't prepared for the _____ face of El Capitan.

180. She decided that a rigid exercise regimen would firm her _____ arms and legs.

Answers

161. *Malleable* means easily molded, controlled, or pressed into shape.

162. *Salutary* means having or producing a beneficial effect.

163. *Florid* means elaborate or ornate.

164. *Pristine* means in its original and unspoiled condition.

165. *Abysmal* means extremely bad.

166. Something *precarious* is fraught with danger.

167. Something *mundane* is dull or routine; without excitement.

168. *Tenuous* means unsubstantial or flimsy.

169. *Askew* means crooked; not straight or level.

170. *Rakish* means debonair; smartly dressed or mannered.

171. *Hermetic* means having an airtight closure; protected from outside influences.

172. *Quiescent* means inactive, quiet, or at rest.

173. *Replete* means well-stocked or abundantly supplied.

174. *Sodden* means thoroughly saturated; soaked.

175. *Amorphous* objects have no definite shape or form.

176. *Fecund* means fertile.

177. *Ad hoc* means for a specific, often temporary, purpose.

178. Something *sinuous* is winding or serpentine.

179. *Precipitous* means extremely steep.

180. *Flaccid* means hanging loose; weak, flabby, not firm.

10

Person, Place, or Thing? Nouns I

Do you often find yourself waiting in a long *queue*? Would time pass faster if you were waiting next to someone who had a great deal of *élan?* The 20 words in this chapter describe interesting people, places, things, or ideas. You can find the answers to each question in this section at the end of the chapter.

Word List

ado (ă·ˈdoo) *n.* fuss, trouble, bother. *Without much ado, she completed her book report.*

amulet (ˈam·yŭ·lit) *n.* something worn around the neck as a charm against evil. *The princess wore an amulet after being cursed by a wizard.*

aperture (ˈap·ĕr·chŭr) *n.* an opening or gap, especially one that lets in light. *The aperture setting on a camera has to be set perfectly to ensure that pictures will have enough light.*

archetype (ˈahr·ki·tīp) *n.* an original model from which others are copied; original pattern or prototype. *Elvis Presley served as the archetype for rock and roll performers in the 1950s.*

bravado (bră·ˈvah·doh) *n.* false courage; a show of pretended bravery. *Kyle's bravado often got him in trouble with other kids in the neighborhood.*

conclave (ˈkon·klav) *n.* a private or secret meeting. *The double agent had a conclave with the spy he was supposed to be observing.*

countenance (ˈkown·tĕ·năns) *n.* the appearance of a person's face, facial features, and expression. *As she walked down the aisle, Julia's countenance was absolutely radiant.*

dichotomy (dī·ˈkot·ŏ·mee) *n.* division into two usually contradictory parts or kinds. *The dichotomy between vanilla ice cream lovers and chocolate ice cream lovers was clear.*

élan (ay·ˈlahn) *n.* 1. vivacity, enthusiasm, vigor. 2. distinctive style or flair. *The new designer's élan and originality was sure to help him succeed in the highly competitive fashion industry.*

ethos (ˈee·thos) *n.* the spirit, attitude, disposition, or beliefs characteristic of a community, epoch, region, etc. *The ethos of their group included a commitment to pacifism.*

harbinger (ˈhahr·bin·jĕr) *n.* a person, thing, or event that foreshadows or indicates what is to come; a forerunner or precursor. *The arrival of the robins is a harbinger of spring.*

impasse (ˈim·pas) *n.* a deadlock, stalemate; a difficulty without a solution. *The labor negotiations with management reached an impasse, and a strike seemed imminent.*

mélange (may·ˈlahnzh) *n.* a mixture or assortment. *There was a very interesting mélange of people at the party.*

nexus (′nek·sŭs) *n.* 1. a means of connection; a link or tie between a series of things 2. a connected series or group 3. the core or center. *The nexus between the lobbyists and the recent policy changes is clear.*

non sequitur (non·′sek·wi·tŭr) *n.* a conclusion that does not logically follow from the evidence. *Marcus's argument started off strong, but it degenerated into a series of non sequiturs.*

pallor (′pal·ŏr) *n.* paleness, lack of color. *The fever subsided, but her pallor remained for several weeks.*

paradigm (′par·ă·dīm) *n.* 1. something that serves as a model or example. 2. set of assumptions, beliefs, values, or practices that constitutes a way of understanding or doing things. *Elected "Employee of the Month," Winona is a paradigm of efficiency.*

pundit (′pun·dit) *n.* a learned person or scholar; one who is an authority on a subject. *The journalist consulted several legal pundits before drafting the article.*

queue (kyoo) *n.* 1. a line of people or vehicles waiting their turn. 2. a pigtail. *Look how long the queue is! We'll be waiting for hours.*

surrogate (′sur·ŏ·git) *n.* a substitute; one who takes the place of another. *Martha agreed to be a surrogate mother for her sister, who could not carry her own child to term.*

For numbers 181–190, select the best <u>synonym</u> in Column B for each vocabulary word in Column A. Circle the correct answer. (If you do not own this book, please write your answers on a separate piece of paper.)

Column A   **Column B**

181. harbinger   **a.** forerunner   **b.** harbor   **c.** convert

182. amulet   **a.** potion   **b.** charm   **c.** anklet

183. pundit   **a.** expert   **b.** politician **c.** kicker

184. paradigm   **a.** example   **b.** timely   **c.** law

185. archetype   **a.** copy   **b.** ancient   **c.** original

186. ethos   **a.** ancient   **b.** spirit   **c.** height

187. queue   **a.** soft   **b.** line   **c.** quick

188. élan   **a.** spirited   **b.** speed   **c.** effective

189. non sequitur   **a.** secret   **b.** clarity   **c.** illogic

190. countenance   **a.** value   **b.** expression **c.** royal

For numbers 191–200, select the best <u>antonym</u> in Column B for each vocabulary word in Column A. Circle the correct answer. (If you do not own this book, please write your answers on a separate piece of paper.)

Column A   **Column B**

191. aperture   **a.** opening   **b.** closure   **c.** huge

192. surrogate   **a.** copy   **b.** survivor   **c.** original

193. conclave   **a.** cave   **b.** secretive   **c.** public meeting

194. bravado   **a.** courage   **b.** cowardice   **c.** scorn

195. pallor   **a.** sick   **b.** color   **c.** bland

196. nexus   **a.** discord   **b.** disconnect **c.** empty

197. dichotomy   **a.** unity   **b.** division   **c.** dissection

198. mélange   **a.** mix   **b.** dessert   **c.** sameness

199. ado   **a.** trouble   **b.** calm   **c.** language

200. impasse   **a.** resolution   **b.** stalemate   **c.** dangerous

Answers

181. **a.** *forerunner.* A *harbinger* is a person or thing that foreshadows a coming event; a precursor.

182. **b.** *charm.* An *amulet* is a charm worn around the neck to ward off evil.

183. **a.** *expert.* A *pundit* is a person who is an authority or expert on a given subject.

184. **a.** *example.* A *paradigm* is a recognized example or model; a standard.

185. **c.** *original.* An *archetype* is an original from which other things are copied.

186. **b.** *spirit.* *Ethos* is a distinguishing spirit, attitude, disposition, or set of beliefs held by a particular person, community, or culture.

187. **b.** *line.* A *queue* is a line, usually of people or vehicles.

188. **a.** *spirited.* *Élan* means vivacity, enthusiasm; it can also mean distinct style or flair.

189. **c.** *illogic.* A *non sequitur* is a conclusion that does not follow a logical path.

190. **b.** *expression.* *Countenance* refers to a person's facial features or expression.

191. **b.** *closure.* An *aperture* is an opening or gap.

192. **c.** *original.* A *surrogate* is something that takes the place of another; a substitute for the original.

193. **c.** *public meeting.* A *conclave* is a secretive meeting.

194. **a.** *courage.* *Bravado* is false courage or pride.

195. **b.** *color.* *Pallor* is paleness or lack of color.

196. **b.** *disconnect. Nexus* is a link or tie between a series of things.

197. **a.** *unity.* A *dichotomy* is a division into two parts, usually contradictory.

198. **c.** *sameness.* A *mélange* is a mixture or assortment of things.

199. **b.** *calm. Ado* is trouble, fuss, or bother.

200. **a.** *resolution.* An *impasse* is a deadlock or stalemate; a resolution would dissolve an impasse.

11

Words about Work and Play, Food and Drink, and Time

Do you prefer food that is bland or food that is *pungent?* Do you have any *quotidian* habits, such as a daily walk? The 20 words in this chapter have to do with work and play, food and drink, and matters of time. You can find the answers to each question in this section at the end of the chapter.

Word List

anachronism (ă·'nak·rŏ·niz·ĕm) *n.* 1. something that is placed into an incorrect historical period. 2. a person, custom, or idea that is out of date. *The authenticity and credibility of the 1920s movie was damaged by the many anachronisms that appeared throughout the scenes.*

archaic (ahr·'kay·ik) *adj.* belonging to former or ancient times; characteristic of the past. *Samantha laughed at her grandfather's archaic views of dating and relationships.*

arduous ('ahr·joo·ŭs) *adj.* 1. very difficult, laborious; requiring great effort. 2. difficult to traverse or surmount. *Commander Shackleton's arduous journey through the Arctic has become the subject of many books and movies.*

coeval (koh·'ee·văl) *adj.* of the same time period; contemporary. *The growth of personal computers and CD players was coeval during the twentieth century.*

cornucopia (kor·nyŭ·'koh·pi·ă) *n.* abundance; a horn of plenty. *The first-graders made cornucopias for Thanksgiving by placing papier-mâché vegetables into a hollowed-out horn.*

dilatory ('dil·ă·tohr·ee) *adj.* slow or late in doing something; intended to delay, especially to gain time. *Resentful for having to work the holiday, Miguel's dilatory approach to getting himself up and dressed was his own small act of passive resistance.*

epicurean (ep·i·'kyoor·i·ăn) *n.* a person devoted to the pursuit of pleasure and luxury, especially the enjoyment of good food and comfort. *While on vacation at a posh resort hotel, Joan became a true epicurean.*

lucrative ('loo·kră·tiv) *adj.* profitable, producing much money. *Teaching is a very rewarding career, but unfortunately it is not very lucrative.*

malinger (mă·'ling·gĕr) *v.* to pretend to be injured or ill in order to avoid work. *Stop malingering and give me a hand with this job.*

onus ('oh·nŭs) *n.* duty or responsibility of doing something; task, burden. *It was Clark's idea, so the onus is on him to show us that it will work.*

perfunctory (pĕr·'fungk·tŏ·ree) *adj.* done out of a sense of duty or routine but without much care or interest; superficial, not thorough. *We were not satisfied with his perfunctory work; we felt a more thorough job could have been done.*

primeval (prī·'mee·văl) *adj.* ancient, original; belonging to the earliest ages. *The primeval art found in the caves was discovered by accident.*

proletariat (proh·lĕ·ˈtair·i·ăt) *n.* the working class; those who do manual labor to earn a living. *The proletariats demanded fewer hours and better wages.*

pungent (ˈpun·jĕnt) *adj.* 1. having a strong, sharp taste or smell. 2. penetrating, caustic; stinging. *I love the pungent taste of a good, strong curry.*

quaff (kwahf) *v.* to drink hurriedly or heartily; to swallow in large draughts. *He quickly quaffed three glasses of water.*

quotidian (kwoh·ˈtid·i·ăn) *adj.* 1. daily. 2. commonplace, pedestrian. *Prudence took her quotidian dose of medicine.*

regale (ri·ˈgayl) *v.* to delight or entertain with a splendid feast or pleasant amusement. *The king regaled his guests until the early morning hours.*

repose (ri·ˈpohz) *n.* 1. resting or being at rest. 2. calmness, tranquility; peace of mind. *The wail of a police siren disturbed my repose.*

slake (slayk) *v.* 1. to satisfy, quench. 2. to reduce the intensity of, moderate, allay. *The deer slaked its thirst at the river.*

toil (toil) 1. *n.* exhausting labor or effort; difficult or laborious work. 2. *v.* to work laboriously, labor strenuously. *Evan toiled for hours before solving the problem.*

For numbers 201–220, read the sentences below carefully. Choose the word from the word list above that best completes the sentence. Write the correct answer in the blank. (If you do not own this book, please write your answers on a separate piece of paper.)

201. With 11 children to care for, Mrs. Higgins had to _____ for many hours just to keep up with the laundry.

202. Suzanne's boss suspected that she was _____ (ing) when she called in sick on Monday morning.

203. Maude's Internet business was so _____ that she was able to retire at the age of 45.

204. Observing Malik sleeping in his hammock by the river on a beautiful summer day, I envied his _____.

205. Boot camp for a U.S. Marine requires _____ training.

206. Since Matthew was the one who wanted the dog, the _____ was on him to walk the dog every morning.

207. The cashier's _____ comment, "Have a nice day," lacked sincerity.

208. Because everyone in Peter's family was a _____, Peter felt both proud and unique because he was the first in his family to go to college.

209. The woman on the corner wearing love beads, a headband, and a jacket with a huge peace symbol on the back is a(n) _____ in the new millennium.

210. Every autumn, Deborah's great-grandmother spends days performing the _____ act of canning fruits for winter, even though she can buy them in the supermarket.

211. The Museum of Natural History has a broad array of archeological displays from contemporary society to _____ artifacts from the age of the caveman.

212. The doctor said that grandpa's _____ walks in the woods were a factor in his living to be 110 years old.

213. Doug was _____ in cleaning up the sports equipment on the field so that he would be there when the cheerleaders came out to practice.

214. The centerpiece of the Thanksgiving dinner table was a beautiful _____ overflowing with fruits and vegetables.

215. Human beings and dinosaurs did not exist during the same time periods; therefore, they were not _____.

216. When Maria finished the marathon, she immediately began to _____ large amounts of water.

217. Miriam was quite a hostess and would _____ her dinner party guests with sumptuous feasts.

218. Mario is a true _____: He is always shopping in the local gourmet food store, sampling new items and stocking his pantry with exquisite foods.

219. In the early 1900s, the Lower East Side in New York City was famous for pickle shops and the _____ odor they gave the neighborhood.

220. According to the legend, the vampire needed to _____ his thirst for blood every night with a new victim.

Answers

201. To *toil* is to do exhausting or very difficult labor.

202. To *malinger* is to pretend to be sick or injured to avoid work.

203. Something *lucrative* produces a lot of money.

204. To be in a state of *repose* is to be at rest and tranquil.

205. Something *arduous* is very difficult and requires tremendous effort.

206. An *onus* is a responsibility or obligation to do something.

207. Something done in a *perfunctory* manner is done in a superficial way, without much care or sincerity.

208. *Proletariat* refers to the working class (e.g. manual laborers).

209. An *anachronism* is something or someone that seems out of place because it seems to be from another era.

210. Something *archaic* belongs to a former or ancient time period.

211. Something *primeval* belongs to or is from the earliest ages.

212. *Quotidian* refers to a daily occurrence or activity.

213. To be *dilatory* is to be slow in doing something, usually to cause a delay or gain time for another purpose.

214. A *cornucopia* (also called horn of plenty) is a hollow, horn-shaped decorative item filled with fruits and vegetables used to symbolize abundance.

215. To be *coeval* means to have existed at the same time; to be contemporaries.

216. To *quaff* means to drink both hurriedly and heartily.

217. To *regale* means to delight or entertain with a splendid feast or pleasant amusement.

218. An *epicurean* is a person devoted to the pursuit of pleasure and luxury, especially the enjoyment of good food and comfort.

219. Something *pungent* has a very strong smell or taste.

220. To *slake* means to satisfy or quench.

12

Opposites Attract—
Antonyms I

Are you a *laconic* person of few words, or do you tend to be *verbose* and talk a lot? The 20 words in this chapter include ten pairs of antonyms. You can find the answers to each question in this section at the end of the chapter.

Word List

allay (ă·ˈlay) *v.* 1. to reduce the intensity of; alleviate. 2. to calm, put to rest. *The CEO's remarks did not allay the concerns of the employees.*

belie (bi·ˈlī) *v.* 1. to give a false impression; misrepresent. 2. to show to be false, to contradict. *By wearing an expensive suit and watch, Alan hoped to belie his lack of success to everyone at the reunion.*

buoyant (ˈboi·ănt) *adj.* 1. able to float. 2. lighthearted, cheerful. *In science class, the children tried to identify which objects on the table would be buoyant.*

credulous (ˈkrej·ŭ·lŭs) *adj.* gullible, too willing to believe things. *Elle's credulous teacher believed her when she told him that the dog ate her homework.*

disabuse (dis·ă·ˈbyooz) *v.* to undeceive, to correct a false impression or erroneous belief. *Natalie needed to disabuse Chin of his belief that she was in love with him.*

disconsolate (dis·ˈkon·sŏ·lit) *adj.* 1. sad, dejected, disappointed. 2. inconsolable, hopelessly unhappy. *The disconsolate look on Peter's face revealed that the letter contained bad news.*

disingenuous (dis·in·ˈjen·yoo·ŭs) *adj.* 1. insincere, calculating; not straightforward or frank. 2. falsely pretending to be unaware. *Carl's disingenuous comments were not taken seriously by anyone in the room.*

exacerbate (ig·ˈzas·ĕr·bayt) *v.* to make worse; to increase the severity, violence, or bitterness of. *We should have known that splashing salt water on Dan's wound would exacerbate his pain.*

incredulous (in·ˈkrej·ŭ·lŭs) *adj.* skeptical, unwilling to believe. *The members of the jury were incredulous when they heard the defendant's far-fetched explanation of the crime.* Note: Do not confuse with *incredible*, meaning "implausible or beyond belief."

ingenuous (in·ˈjen·yoo·ŭs) *adj.* 1. not cunning or deceitful; unable to mask feelings; artless, frank, sincere. 2. lacking sophistication or worldliness. *Donald's expression of regret was ingenuous, for even though he didn't know her well, he felt a deep sadness when Mary died.* Note: Do not confuse with *ingenious*, meaning "remarkably clever."

intrepid (in·ˈtrep·id) *adj.* fearless, brave, undaunted. *The intrepid nature and fortitude of the U.S. Marines is legendary.*

jocund (ˈjok·ŭnd) *adj.* merry, cheerful; sprightly and lighthearted. *Alex's jocund nature makes it a pleasure to be near her.*

laconic (lă·ˈkon·ik) *adj.* brief, to the point; terse. *A man of few words, Morrison gave a ten-minute commencement address that was everything we could have asked for: laconic, powerful, and inspirational.*

lugubrious (luu·ˈgoo·bri·ŭs) *adj.* excessively dismal or mournful, often exaggeratedly or ridiculously so. *Billy looks like a fool, acting so lugubrious over losing a silly bet.*

nadir (ˈnay·dĭr) *n.* the very bottom, the lowest point. *When he felt he was at the nadir of his life, Robert began to practice mediation to elevate his spirits.*

spurious (ˈspyoor·i·ŭs) *adj.* false, counterfeit; not genuine or authentic. *The expert confirmed that the Willie Mays autograph was spurious.*

timorous (ˈtim·ŏ·rŭs) *adj.* fearful, timid, afraid. *The stray dog was timorous, and it took a great deal of coaxing to get him to come near the car.*

verbose (vĕr·ˈbohs) *adj.* using more words than necessary; wordy, long-winded. *Her verbose letter rambled so much that it didn't seem to have a point.*

veritable (ˈver·i·tă·bĕl) *adj.* real, true, genuine. *Einstein was a veritable genius.*

zenith (ˈzee·nith) *n.* 1. the highest point; top, peak. 2. the point in the sky directly above the observer. *She is at the zenith of her legal career, having won every case this year.*

For numbers 221–230, you will find two antonyms paired together at the beginning of each analogy. Choose the set of antonyms that best defines the two vocabulary words and completes the analogy. Circle the letter of the correct answer. (If you do not own this book, please write your answers on a separate piece of paper.)

221. zenith : nadir ::
   a. future : past
   b. inside : outside
   c. wisdom : ignorance
   d. top : bottom

222. disingenuous : ingenuous ::
   a. smart : stupid
   b. deceptive : sincere
   c. banal : avant-garde
   d. effusive : reserved

223. credulous : incredulous ::
   a. real : fake
   b. moral : immoral
   c. gullible : skeptical
   d. plain : exceptional

224. intrepid : timorous ::
   a. large : small
   b. coastal : landlocked
   c. brave : timid
   d. strong : weak

225. disconsolate : buoyant ::
   a. miserable : happy
   b. unconnected : connected
   c. difficult : easy
   d. broken : repaired

226. disabuse : belie ::
   a. aid : attack
   b. immoral : moral
   c. undeceive : deceive
   d. remove : attach

227. veritable : spurious ::
   a. authentic : fake
   b. assembled : scattered
   c. well-known : obscure
   d. meaningful : meaningless

228. allay : exacerbate ::
   a. near : far
   b. right : wrong
   c. even : askew
   d. calm : agitate

229. jocund : lugubrious ::
   a. ignorant : wise
   b. shy : outgoing
   c. sober : drunk
   d. joyous : miserable

230. laconic : verbose ::
   a. slow : fast
   b. concise : long-winded
   c. healthy : ill
   d. discordant : harmonious

For questions 231–240, choose the definition that is most nearly the *opposite* of the selected vocabulary word. The correct answer will be both the vocabulary word's *antonym* and the definition for another word from this chapter. (If you do not own this book, please write your answers on a separate piece of paper.)

231. incredulous
   a. faithful
   b. trustworthy
   c. naive
   d. incredible

232. disabuse
   a. hide the truth
   b. reveal the truth
   c. speak in an abusive manner
   d. praise

233. laconic
   a. lazy
   b. energetic
   c. fleeting
   d. wordy

234. timorous
   a. shy
   b. fearless
   c. trembling
   d. enraged

235. spurious
   a. genuine
   b. antique
   c. not believable
   d. pleasant

236. nadir
   a. highest honor
   b. median
   c. peak
   d. bottomless pit

237. allay
   a. postpone
   b. intensify
   c. relieve
   d. deny

238. jocund
   a. chubby
   b. polite
   c. rude
   d. dismal

239. disingenuous
   a. false
   b. genius
   c. reliable
   d. honest

240. buoyant
   a. very sad
   b. comfortable in water
   c. peaceful
   d. joyful

Answers

221. **d.** *Zenith* is the highest point, top. *Nadir* is the very bottom.

222. **b.** *Disingenuous* means insincere. *Ingenuous* means sincere, free of deceit.

223. **c.** *Credulous* means too willing to believe, gullible. *Incredulous* means skeptical.

224. **c.** *Intrepid* means brave, fearless. *Timorous* means timid and fearful.

225. **a.** *Disconsolate* means sad, disappointed. *Buoyant* means lighthearted and cheerful.

226. **c.** *Disabuse* means to correct a false impression. *Belie* means to mislead or misrepresent.

227. **a.** *Veritable* means real, true, and genuine. *Spurious* means false, counterfeit.

228. **d.** *Allay* means to calm or reassure. *Exacerbate* means to make worse or intensify.

229. **d.** *Jocund* means merry and joyous. *Lugubrious* means excessively miserable.

230. **b.** *Laconic* means concise, brief, and to the point. *Verbose* means long-winded, wordy.

231. **c.** *Incredulous* means skeptical. Its antonym is *credulous*, which means gullible, too willing to believe; naive.

232. **a.** *Disabuse* means to correct a false impression. Its antonym is *belie*, which means to mislead or misrepresent.

233. **d.** *Laconic* means concise, brief, to the point. Its antonym is *verbose*, which means long-winded, wordy.

234. **b.** *Timorous* means timid, fearful. Its antonym is *intrepid*, which means fearless, brave.

235. **a.** *Spurious* means false, counterfeit, or fake. Its antonym is *veritable*, which means real, true, or genuine.

236. **c.** *Nadir* means the lowest point or very bottom. Its antonym is *zenith*, which means the absolute top or peak.

237. **b.** *Allay* means to calm, reassure; to alleviate or reduce in intensity. Its antonym is *exacerbate*, which means to intensify, make worse.

238. **d.** *Jocund* means merry and happy, joyous. Its antonym is *lugubrious*, which means excessively dismal, miserable.

239. **d.** *Disingenuous* means insincere, deceitful. Its antonym is *ingenuous*, which means sincere, not cunning; free of deceit.

240. **a.** *Buoyant* means light-hearted, joyful. Its antonym is *disconsolate*, which means sad, dejected.

13

Describing Ideas and Arguments

Have you ever faced an *inscrutable* problem that you just could not seem to solve? Have you recently enjoyed a particularly *poignant* book or film? The vocabulary words in this chapter will help you better describe ideas and arguments. You can find the answers to each question in this section at the end of the chapter.

Word List

avant-garde (a·vahnt·ˈgahrd) *adj.* using or favoring an ultramodern or experimental style; innovative, cutting-edge, especially in the arts or literature. *Though it seems conventional now, in the 1950s, Andy Warhol's art was viewed as avant-garde.*

cogent (ˈkoh·jĕnt) *adj.* convincing, persuasive; compelling belief. *Ella's cogent arguments helped the debate team win the state championship.*

conciliatory (kŏn·ˈsil·i·ă·tohr·ee) *adj.* making or willing to make concessions to reconcile, soothe, or comfort; mollifying, appeasing. *Abraham Lincoln made conciliatory gestures toward the South at the end of the Civil War.*

derivative (di·ˈriv·ă·tiv) *adj.* derived from another source; unoriginal. *The word "atomic" is a derivative of the word "atom."*

desultory (ˈdes·ŭl·tohr·ee) *adj.* aimless, haphazard; moving from one subject to another without logical connection. *The family became concerned listening to their grandmother's desultory ramblings.*

dogmatic (dawg·ˈmat·ik) *adj.* 1. asserting something in a positive, absolute, arrogant way. 2. of or relating to dogma. *The professor's dogmatic style of conversation was not very popular with his young students.*

edifying (ˈed·ĭ·fī·ing) *adj.* enlightening or uplifting with the aim of improving intellectual or moral development; instructing, improving. *His edifying sermon challenged the congregation to devote more time to charitable causes.*

efficacious (ef·ĭ·ˈkay·shŭs) *adj.* acting effectively, producing the desired effect or result. *Margaret's efficacious approach to her job in the collections department made her a favorite with the CFO.*

incendiary (in·ˈsen·di·er·ee) *adj.* 1. causing or capable of causing fire; burning readily. 2. of or involving arson. 3. tending to incite or inflame; inflammatory. *Fire marshals checked for incendiary devices in the theater after they received an anonymous warning.*

inscrutable (in·ˈscroo·tă·bĕl) *adj.* baffling, unfathomable; incapable of being understood. *It was completely inscrutable how the escape artist got out of the trunk.*

involute (ˈin·vŏ·loot) *adj.* intricate, complex. *The tax reform committee faces an extremely involute problem if it wants to distribute the tax burden equally.*

lucid ('loo·sid) *adj.* 1. very clear, easy to understand; intelligible 2. sane or rational. *Andrea presented a very lucid argument that proved her point beyond a shadow of a doubt.*

pedantic (pi·'dăn·tik) *adj.* marked by a narrow, tiresome focus on or display of learning, especially of rules or trivial matters. *Her lessons were so pedantic that I found I was easily bored.*

pellucid (pĕ·'loo·sid) *adj.* 1. translucent, able to be seen through with clarity. 2. (e.g., of writing) very clear, easy to understand. *Senator Waterson's pellucid argument made me change my vote.*

poignant ('poin·yănt) *adj.* 1. arousing emotion; deeply moving, touching. 2. keenly distressing; piercing or incisive. *They captured the poignant reunion on film.*

polemical (pŏ·'lem·ik·ăl) *adj.* controversial, argumentative. *The analyst presented a highly polemical view of the economic situation.*

prosaic (proh·'zay·ik) *adj.* unimaginative, ordinary; dull. *The prosaic novel was rejected by the publisher.*

specious ('spee·shŭs) *adj.* 1. seemingly plausible but false. 2. deceptively pleasing in appearance. *Vinnie did not fool me with his specious argument.*

tangible ('tan·jĭ·bĕl) *adj.* able to be perceived by touch; palpable; real or concrete. *There is no tangible evidence of misconduct; it's all hearsay.*

vacuous ('vak·yoo·ŭs) *adj.* empty, purposeless; senseless, stupid, or inane. *This TV show is yet another vacuous sitcom.*

For numbers 241–250, select the best <u>synonym</u> in Column B for each vocabulary word in Column A. Circle the correct answer. (If you do not own this book, please write your answers on a separate piece of paper.)

Column A   **Column B**

241. specious   **a.** special   **b.** misleading   **c.** wide open

242. tangible   **a.** perceptible   **b.** soft   **c.** weak

243. poignant   **a.** good   **b.** exceptional   **c.** moving

244. incendiary   **a.** specific   **b.** flammable   **c.** amazing

245. prosaic   **a.** profound   **b.** banal   **c.** vulgar

246. cogent   **a.** audible   **b.** tasty   **c.** convincing

247. desultory   **a.** focused   **b.** boring   **c.** aimless

248. efficacious   **a.** tidy   **b.** small   **c.** effective

249. inscrutable   **a.** small   **b.** unfathomable   **c.** annoying

250. conciliatory **a.** appeasing   **b.** advising   **c.** pleasant

For numbers 251–260, select the best <u>antonym</u> in Column B for each vocabulary word in Column A. Circle the correct answer. (If you do not own this book, please write your answers on a separate piece of paper.)

Column A   **Column B**

251. polemical   **a.** agreeable   **b.** controversial **c.** political

252. avant-garde   **a.** different   **b.** conventional   **c.** unguarded

253. derivative   **a.** component   **b.** copy   **c.** original

254. involute   **a.** simple   **b.** complex   **c.** painful

255. pellucid   **a.** opaque   **b.** strange   **c.** conventional

256. vacuous   **a.** open   **b.** closed   **c.** meaningful

257. pedantic   **a.** nonstudious   **b.** childlike   **c.** mature

258. edifying   **a.** corrupting   **b.** helping   **c.** enlightening

259. lucid   **a.** awake   **b.** easy   **c.** unclear

260. dogmatic   **a.** unsure   **b.** passionless   **c.** loud

Answers

241. **b.** *misleading.* To be *specious* is to be seemingly plausible but false.

242. **a.** *perceptible.* To be *tangible* is to be perceptible, especially by touch.

243. **c.** *moving.* To be *poignant* is to be deeply moving or emotional.

244. **b.** *flammable.* *Incendiary* means burning readily or inflammatory.

245. **b.** *banal.* To be *prosaic* is to be unimaginative, ordinary, or dull.

246. **c.** *convincing.* *Cogent* means convincing or persuasive.

247. **c.** *aimless.* *Desultory* means aimless, haphazard.

248. **c.** *effective.* To be *efficacious* is to produce a desired effect or result.

249. **b.** *unfathomable.* Something *inscrutable* is baffling; incapable of being understood.

250. **a.** *appeasing.* *Conciliatory* means willing to make concessions to reconcile; mollifying, appeasing.

251. **a.** *agreeable.* To be *polemical* is to be controversial or argumentative.

252. **b.** *conventional.* *Avant-garde* means experimental in style; innovative, or cutting-edge.

253. **c.** *original.* A *derivative* comes from another source; it is unoriginal.

254. **a.** *simple.* *Involute* means complex, intricate.

255. **a.** *opaque.* *Pellucid* means translucent; able to be seen through with clarity.

256. **c.** *meaningful.* To be *vacuous* is to be purposeless, senseless, or stupid.

257. **a.** *nonstudious. Pedantic* means focusing rigidly on learning, especially regarding rules or trivial matters.

258. **a.** *corrupting. Edifying* means to inspire with the goal of improving intellectual or moral development.

259. **c.** *unclear. Lucid* means easily understood, rational.

260. **a.** *unsure. Dogmatic* means asserting something in a positive, absolute, or arrogant way.

14

Things to Do—More Useful Verbs

Did you ever *forswear* a bad habit only to find you couldn't break it? Have you ever *dissuaded* someone from doing something dangerous? The 20 verbs in this chapter offer more expressive ways to describe actions. You can find the answers to each question in this section at the end of the chapter.

Word List

abstain (ab·ˈstayn) *v.* to choose to refrain from doing something, especially to refrain from voting. *I have decided to abstain from drinking alcohol.*

ameliorate (ă·ˈmeel·yŏ·rayt) *v.* to make or become better; to improve. *The diplomat was able to ameliorate the tense situation between the two nations.*

appease (ă·ˈpeez) *v.* to make calm or quiet, soothe; to still or pacify. *His ability to appease his constituents helped him become reelected.*

apprise (ă·ˈprīz) *v.* to inform, give notice to. *Part of Susan's job as a public defender was to apprise people of their legal rights.*

appropriate (ă·ˈproh·pree·ayt) *v.* to take for one's own use, often without permission; to set aside for a special purpose. *The state legislature will appropriate two million dollars from the annual budget to build a new bridge on the interstate highway.*

assay (ă·ˈsay) *v.* 1. to try, put to a test. 2. to examine. 3. to judge critically, evaluate after an analysis. *The chief engineer wanted a laboratory to assay the steel before using it in the construction project.*

delineate (di·ˈlin·i·ayt) *v.* to draw or outline, sketch; to portray, depict, or describe. *The survey will clearly delineate where their property ends.*

demur (di·ˈmur) *v.* to raise objections, hesitate. *Polly hated to demur, but she didn't think adding ten cloves of garlic to the recipe was a good idea.*

disconcert (dis·kŏn·ˈsurt) *v.* 1. to upset the composure of, ruffle. 2. to frustrate plans by throwing into disorder. *The arrival of her ex-husband and his new wife managed to disconcert the typically unflappable Miriam.*

dissemble (di·ˈsem·bĕl) *v.* to disguise or conceal one's true feelings or motives behind a false appearance. *Tom needed to dissemble his goal of taking his boss's job by acting supportive of his boss's planned job change.*

dissuade (di·ˈswayd) *v.* to discourage from, or persuade against, a course of action. *I tried to dissuade them from painting their house purple, but they didn't listen.*

dither (ˈdi*th*·ĕr) *v.* 1. to hesitate; to be indecisive and uncertain. 2. to shake or quiver. *During a crisis, it is important to have a leader who will not dither.*

divulge (dī·ˈvulj) *v.* to disclose; to make something known that may have been private or secret. *The reporter refused to divulge her source.*

evince (i·'vins) *v.* to show or demonstrate clearly; to make evident. *The algebra teacher tried to evince the complexity of the material to be covered on the midterm.*

extenuate (iks·'ten·yoo·ayt) *v.* to reduce the strength or lessen the seriousness of; to try to partially excuse. *Fred claimed that extenuating circumstances forced him to commit forgery.*

forswear (for·'swair) *v.* 1. to give up, renounce. 2. to deny under oath. *Natasha had to forswear her allegiance to her homeland in order to become a citizen of the new country.*

impute (im·'pyoot) *v.* to attribute to a cause or source, ascribe; credit. *Doctors impute the reduction in cancer deaths to the nationwide decrease in cigarette smoking.*

obfuscate (ob·'fus·kayt) *v.* 1. to make obscure or unclear; to muddle or make difficult to understand. 2. to dim or darken. *Instead of clarifying the matter, Walter only obfuscated it further.*

rescind (ri·'sind) *v.* to repeal or cancel; to void or annul. *They have rescinded their offer, so we must find another buyer.*

stymie ('stī·mee) *v.* to hinder, obstruct, or thwart; to prevent the accomplishment of something. *The negotiations were stymied by yet another attack.*

For numbers 261–270, read the following sentences carefully. Decide which answer best describes the italicized vocabulary word in the prompt. Circle the letter of the correct answer. If you do not own this book, please write your answers on a separate piece of paper.

261. If you *abstain* from something, you
   a. run from it.
   b. choose not to do it.
   c. come from it.
   d. have an allergic reaction to it.

262. If you *rescind* an offer, you
   a. make the offer.
   b. revise the offer.
   c. cancel the offer.
   d. increase the offer.

263. If you *forswear* eating chocolate, you
   a. stop eating chocolate.
   b. love eating chocolate.
   c. depend on chocolate.
   d. get sick if you eat chocolate.

264. If you *appease* someone, you
   a. anger that person.
   b. annoy that person.
   c. calm that person.
   d. please that person.

265. If you *delineate* something, you
   a. divide it in two.
   b. draw or describe it.
   c. reverse it.
   d. count or mark it.

266. If you *demur* during a discussion, you
   a. raise an objection.
   b. make a good point.
   c. make an embarrassing remark.
   d. say something that insults someone.

267. If you *disconcert* someone, you
    a. make that person late for something.
    b. make that person happy.
    c. upset that person's composure.
    d. recognize that person.

268. If you *dissuade* someone, you
    a. discourage that person from doing something.
    b. deceive that person.
    c. reveal a secret to that person.
    d. disappoint that person.

269. If you *stymie* someone's plans, you
    a. copy those plans.
    b. change those plans.
    c. cancel those plans.
    d. obstruct those plans.

270. If you *assay* something, you
    a. buy it.
    b. examine it.
    c. declare it.
    d. borrow it.

For questions 271–280, read the sentences below carefully. Decide which vocabulary word best matches the action described in the sentence. Circle the letter of the correct answer. (If you do not own this book, please write your answers on a separate piece of paper.)

271. Tammy drastically improved the situation.
    a. evince
    b. demur
    c. ameliorate
    d. rescind

272. Ryan hid his plans to steal Jason's girlfriend behind a mask of false friendship.
    a. obfuscate
    b. appropriate
    c. dissemble
    d. disconcert

273. Ian attributed the rent increase to the new sports complex downtown.
   a. impute
   b. ameliorate
   c. extenuate
   d. divulge

274. Darlene's lack of serious injury made the benefits of using a seatbelt very clear.
   a. apprise
   b. evince
   c. dissuade
   d. dither

275. Carson's problems at home made his boss overlook his sloppy work.
   a. appropriate
   b. divulge
   c. rescind
   d. extenuate

276. The general informed the president of the latest events.
   a. obfuscate
   b. apprise
   c. ameliorate
   d. impute

277. The funds were put aside to build a computer laboratory for the students.
   a. dither
   b. abstain
   c. appropriate
   d. evince

278. Casey's version of the story only made it even more unclear how the accident happened.
   a. obfuscate
   b. extenuate
   c. stymie
   d. dissemble

279. Carmella told the entire office about the boss's scandalous affair.
   a. dissuade
   b. divulge
   c. apprise
   d. appease

280. Dina wasn't sure which class to register for and caused a delay for others waiting in line.
   a. abstain
   b. divulge
   c. obfuscate
   d. dither

Answers

261. **b.** To *abstain* means to choose to refrain from doing something.

262. **c.** To *rescind* means to repeal or cancel; to void or annul.

263. **a.** To *forswear* means to stop, give up, or renounce. It can also mean to deny under oath.

264. **c.** To *appease* means to make calm or quiet; to soothe, still, or pacify.

265. **b.** To *delineate* means to draw or outline; to portray or describe.

266. **a.** To *demur* means to raise an objection.

267. **c.** To *disconcert* means to upset the composure of; to frustrate plans by throwing into disorder.

268. **a.** To *dissuade* means to discourage from or persuade against a course of action.

269. **d.** To *stymie* means to hinder, obstruct, or thwart; to prevent the accomplishment of something.

270. **b.** To *assay* means to test or try; to examine; or to judge critically.

271. **c.** To *ameliorate* means to make or become better; to improve.

272. **c.** To *dissemble* means to disguise or conceal one's true feelings or motives behind a false appearance.

273. **a.** To *impute* means to attribute to a cause or source; to ascribe or credit.

274. **b.** To *evince* means to show or demonstrate clearly; to make evident.

275. **d.** To *extenuate* means to reduce the strength or lessen the seriousness of; to try to partially excuse.

276. **b.** To *apprise* means to inform; to give notice to.

277. **c.** To *appropriate* means to set aside for a special purpose. It can also mean to take for one's own use, often without permission.

278. **a.** To *obfuscate* means to make obscure or unclear, to muddle or make difficult to understand. It can also mean to dim or darken.

279. **b.** To *divulge* means to make known; to make public.

280. **d.** To *dither* means to hesitate, to be indecisive or uncertain. It can also mean to shake or quiver.

15

Word Pairs III

Were you ever given a gift that you would never wear because it was too *garish* or *tawdry*? Do you avoid *pugnacious* or *belligerent* people because you do not like to fight? This is the third of four chapters of *word pairs*—pairs of words that are almost exactly the same in meaning. Each word pair chapter contains ten sets of synonyms. You can find the answers to each question in this section at the end of the chapter.

Word List

antipathy (an·'tip·ă·thee) *n.* 1. a strong aversion or dislike. 2. an object of aversion. *The seven year old had a great antipathy toward green vegetables.*

apropos (ap·rŏ·'poh) *adj.* appropriate to the situation; suitable to what is being said or done. *The chairman's remarks referring to the founding fathers were apropos, since it was the Fourth of July.*

assuage (ă·'swayj) *v.* to make something less severe, to soothe; to satisfy (as hunger or thirst). *The small cups of water offered to the marathon runners helped to assuage their thirst.*

attenuate (ă·'ten·yoo·ayt) *v.* 1. to make thin or slender. 2. to weaken; to reduce in force, value, or degree. *The Russian army was able to attenuate the strength and number of the German forces by leading them inland during winter.*

auspicious (aw·'spish·ŭs) *adj.* favorable, showing signs of promise success; propitious. *Valerie believed it an auspicious beginning when it rained on the day that she opened her umbrella store.*

aversion (ă·'vur·zhŏn) *n.* 1. a strong, intense dislike; repugnance. 2. the object of this feeling. *Todd has an aversion to arugula and picks it out of his salads.*

belligerent (bi·'lij·ĕr·ĕnt) *adj.* hostile and aggressive, showing an eagerness to fight. *Mrs. Rivera always kept an eye on Daniel during recess because his belligerent attitude often caused problems with other children.*

enervate ('en·ĕr·vayt) *v.* to weaken; deprive of strength or vitality; to make feeble or impotent. *Stephanie's cutting remarks managed to enervate Hasaan.*

equanimity (ee·kwă·'nim·i·tee) *n.* calmness of temperament, even-temperedness; patience and composure, especially under stressful circumstances. *The hostage negotiator's equanimity during the standoff was remarkable.*

eradicate (i·'rad·ĭ·kayt) *v.* to root out and utterly destroy; to annihilate, exterminate. *The exterminator said he would eradicate the vermin from the house.*

expunge (ik·'spunj) *v.* to wipe or rub out, delete; to eliminate completely, annihilate. *After finishing probation, juveniles can petition the courts to expunge their criminal records.*

felicitous (fi·'lis·i·tŭs) *adj.* 1. apt, suitably expressed; apropos. 2. marked by good fortune. *The felicitous turn of events during her promotional tour propelled Susan's book to the best-seller list.*

garish (ˈgair·ish) *adj.* excessively bright or overdecorated; gaudy; tastelessly showy. *Though Susan thought Las Vegas was garish, Emily thought it was perfectly beautiful.*

mollify (ˈmol·ĭ·fī) *v.* 1. to soothe the anger of, to calm. 2. to lessen in intensity. 3. to soften, make less rigid. *The crying child was quickly mollified by her mother.*

ostracize (ˈos·tră·sīz) *v.* to reject, cast out from a group or from society. *Kendall was ostracized after he repeatedly stole from his friends.*

pariah (pă·ˈrī·ă) *n.* an outcast; a rejected and despised person. *After he told a sexist joke, Jason was treated like a pariah by all of the women in the office.*

propitious (proh·ˈpish·ŭs) *adj.* auspicious, presenting favorable circumstances. *These are propitious omens indeed and foretell a good journey.*

pugnacious (pug·ˈnay·shŭs) *adj.* contentious, quarrelsome; eager to fight, belligerent. *Don't be so pugnacious—I don't want to fight.*

sangfroid (sahn·ˈfrwah) *n.* composure, especially in dangerous or difficult circumstances. *I wish I had Jane's sangfroid when I find myself in a confrontational situation.*

tawdry (ˈtaw·dree) *adj.* gaudy or showy but without any real value; flashy and tasteless. *I've never seen such a tawdry outfit as the three-tiered taffeta prom gown that the singer wore to the awards ceremony!*

Crossword Puzzle Directions

In this puzzle, there is one clue for each set of synonyms, so each clue is offered twice. Read the definition provided in the clue and determine which two words share that meaning. Then, determine which of those synonyms fits the designated crossword squares. (Note: All pairs are the same part of speech, except one pair which is a verb and a noun.)

Word Pairs III Crossword Puzzle

ACROSS

283. calmness and composure, especially under stress (paired with 292 down)

285. to weaken; reduce in strength or force (paired with 282 down)

287. intense dislike (paired with 281 down)

288. appropriate, suitable for the situation (paired with 284 down)

291. hostile, eager to fight (paired with 295 across)

295. hostile, eager to fight (paired with 291 across)

296. an outcast or rejected person (noun); to reject or cast out from society (verb) (paired with 300 across)

298. to soothe; to lessen in intensity (paired with 294 down)

299. to destroy completely; annihilate (paired with 293 down)

300. to reject or cast out from society (verb); an outcast or rejected person (noun) (paired with 296 across)

DOWN

281. intense dislike (paired with 287 across)

282. to weaken; reduce in strength or force (paired with 285 across)

284. appropriate, suitable for the situation (paired with 288 across)

286. favorable; presenting favorable circumstances (paired with 289 down)

289. favorable; presenting favorable circumstances (paired with 286 down)

290. extremely showy; flashy and tasteless (paired with 297 down)

292. calmness and composure, especially under stress (paired with 283 across)

293. to destroy completely; annihilate (paired with 299 across)

294. to soothe; to lessen in intensity (paired with 298 across)

297. extremely showy; flashy and tasteless (paired with 290 down)

Answers

The following words are *word pairs*:

antipathy, aversion
apropos, felicitous
assuage, mollify
attenuate, enervate
belligerent, pugnacious
equanimity, sangfroid
eradicate, expunge
garish, tawdry
ostracize, pariah
propitious, auspicious

Across

283. *Sangfroid* means composure, especially in dangerous or difficult circumstances; *equanimity*.

285. To *attenuate* means to weaken; to reduce in force, value, or degree; *enervate*. It also means to make thin or slender.

287. *Antipathy* is a strong *aversion* or dislike.

288. *Apropos* means appropriate to the situation, suitable to what is being said or done; felicitous.

291. *Belligerent* means hostile and aggressive, showing an eagerness to fight; *pugnacious*.

295. *Pugnacious* means contentious, quarrelsome, eager to fight; *belligerent*.

296. A *pariah* (noun) is an outcast, a rejected, and despised person; someone who has been *ostracized* (verb).

298. To *mollify* is to soothe the anger of, calm, *assuage*; to lessen in intensity; or to soften, make less rigid.

299. To *eradicate* means to root out and utterly destroy, to annihilate; to *expunge*.

300. To *ostracize* (verb) is to reject, to cast out from a group or from society; someone who has been ostracized is a *pariah* (noun).

Down

281. An *aversion* is a strong, intense dislike; repugnance, *antipathy*.

282. To *enervate* is to weaken, to deprive of strength or vitality, to *attenuate*; to make feeble or impotent.

284. *Felicitous* means apt, suitably expressed; *apropos*. It also means marked by good fortune.

286. *Auspicious* means favorable; showing signs that promise success, *propitious*.

289. *Propitious* means *auspicious*, presenting favorable circumstances.

290. *Garish* means excessively bright or over-decorated, gaudy; tastelessly showy, *tawdry*.

292. *Equanimity* means calmness of temperament, even-temperedness; patience and composure, especially under stressful circumstances; *sangfroid*.

293. To *expunge* is to wipe or rub out, delete; to eliminate completely, annihilate, *eradicate*.

294. To *assuage* is to make something less severe, to soothe, *mollify*; to satisfy.

297. *Tawdry* means gaudy or showy but without any real value; flashy and tasteless, *garish*.

16

Personality Traits and Attitudes II

Do you often make people laugh with your *facetious* remarks? Have you ever been *flippant* when you should have been more serious? Here are 20 more words that describe who we are and how we behave. You can find the answers to each question in this section at the end of the chapter.

Word List

adamant ('ad·ă·mănt) *adj.* 1. unyielding to requests, appeals, or reason. 2. firm, inflexible. *The senator was adamant that no changes would be made to the defense budget.*

apathetic (ap·ă·'thet·ik) *adj.* feeling or showing a lack of interest, concern, or emotion; indifferent, unresponsive. *Mrs. Brownstone was distressed by how apathetic her eighth grade students were about world history.*

ascetic (ă·'set·ik) *adj.* practicing self-denial, not allowing oneself pleasures or luxuries; austere. *Some religions require their leaders to lead an ascetic lifestyle as an example to their followers.*

audacious (aw·'day·shŭs) *adj.* fearlessly or recklessly daring or bold; unrestrained by convention or propriety. *Detective Malloy's methods were considered bold and audacious by his superiors, and they often achieved results.*

complaisant (kŏm·'play·sănt) *adj.* tending to comply; obliging, willing to do what pleases others. *To preserve family peace and harmony, Lenny became very complaisant when his in-laws came to visit.*

ebullient (i·'bul·yěnt) *adj.* bubbling over with enthusiasm, exuberant. *The ebullient children were waiting to stick their hands into the grab bag and pull out a toy.*

facetious (fă·'see·shŭs) *adj.* humorous and witty, cleverly amusing; jocular, sportive. *Mr. Weston's facetious remarks always made people laugh.*

flippant ('flip·ănt) *adj.* not showing proper seriousness; disrespectful, saucy. *Ursula's flippant remarks in front of her fiancé's parents were an embarrassment to us all.*

impassive (im·'pas·iv) *adj.* not showing or feeling emotion or pain. *It was hard to know what she was feeling by looking at the impassive expression on her face.*

imperious (im·'peer·i·ŭs) *adj.* overbearing, bossy, domineering. *Stella was relieved with her new job transfer because she would no longer be under the control of such an imperious boss.*

impetuous (im·'pech·oo·ŭs) *adj.* 1. characterized by sudden, forceful energy or emotion; impulsive, unduly hasty and without thought. 2. marked by violent force. *It was an impetuous decision to run off to Las Vegas and get married after a one-week courtship.*

insouciant (in·ˈsoo·si·ănt) *adj.* unconcerned, carefree, indifferent. *Wendy's insouciant attitude toward her future concerned her father, who expected her to go to college.*

mettlesome (ˈmet·ĕl·sŏm) *adj.* courageous, high-spirited. *Alice's mettlesome attitude was infectious and inspired us all to press on.* Note: Do not confuse with *meddlesome*, meaning *inclined to interfere.*

morose (mo·ˈrohs) *adj.* gloomy, sullen; melancholy. *My daughter has been morose ever since our dog ran away.*

nonchalant (non·shă·ˈlant) *adj.* indifferent or cool, not showing anxiety or excitement. *Franco tried to be nonchalant, but I could tell he was nervous.*

officious (ŏ·ˈfish·ŭs) *adj.* meddlesome, bossy; eagerly offering unnecessary or unwanted advice. *My officious Aunt Midge is coming to the party, so be prepared for lots of questions and advice.*

peremptory (pĕ·ˈremp·tŏ·ree) *adj.* 1. offensively self-assured, dictatorial. 2. commanding, imperative, not allowing contradiction or refusal. 3. putting an end to debate or action. *The mother's peremptory tone ended the children's bickering.*

querulous (ˈkwer·ŭ·lŭs) *adj.* complaining, peevish; discontented. *He's a picky and querulous old man, but I still love him.*

sanctimonious (sangk·tĭ·ˈmoh·nee·ŭs) *adj.* hypocritically pious or devout; excessively self-righteous. *The thief's sanctimonious remark that "a fool and his money are soon parted" only made the jury more eager to convict him.*

vitriolic (vit·ri·ˈol·ik) *adj.* savagely hostile or bitter; caustic. *Her vitriolic attack on her opponent was so hostile that it may cost her the election.*

For numbers 301–310, you will find sentences that describe a personality type or character trait. Read each sentence carefully and then circle the vocabulary word that best describes the person or character trait. (If you do not own this book, please write your answers on a separate piece of paper.)

301. To please her boyfriend, Charlotte changed the way she dressed to a style that he preferred.

Charlotte is being
a. apathetic.
b. flippant.
c. complaisant.
d. impetuous.

302. Although he failed another exam, Ivan didn't seem to care.

Ivan is being
a. adamant.
b. apathetic.
c. querulous.
d. imperious.

303. "It's *my* way or the highway!" said George.

George is being
a. impassive.
b. facetious.
c. morose.
d. peremptory.

304. "My future mother-in-law continually gives me suggestions on planning my wedding. She even ordered the flowers without consulting me first."

The mother-in-law is being
a. officious.
b. flippant.
c. ebullient.
d. complaisant.

305. When working at the scene of an accident, rescue workers often hide their emotions and maintain a professional countenance.

The rescue workers are being
a. audacious.
b. morose.
c. apathetic.
d. impassive.

306. Mistakenly believing his boss was speaking ill of him, Angelo burst through the door and yelled: "I quit!" to his boss.

Angelo was being
a. imperious.
b. ebullient.
c. impetuous.
d. querulous.

307. At the end of his life, the reclusive billionaire lived in a small apartment with a bed and a bible as his only possessions, even though he could have had almost any luxury.

The billionaire chose a lifestyle that was
a. insouciant.
b. morose.
c. ascetic.
d. facetious.

308. Susan absolutely insisted that we come along; she wouldn't take no for an answer.

Susan was being
a. adamant.
b. querulous.
c. peremptory.
d. audacious.

309. Raj was someone who, no matter how perfect the day, would always find something to complain about.

Raj is very
a. nonchalant.
b. vitriolic.
c. officious.
d. querulous.

310. "You fatuous boor! You've ruined my life! I never want to see you again!"

This statement is
a. morose.
b. vitriolic.
c. insouciant.
d. apathetic.

For numbers 311–320, you will find sentences describing a personality trait or attitude followed by a fill in the blank exercise. Read each sentence carefully and choose the vocabulary word from the list below that best completes the second sentence. Write the correct answer in the blank. (If you do not own this book, please write your answers on a separate piece of paper.)

audacious	insouciant
ebullient	mettlesome
facetious	morose
flippant	nonchalant
imperious	sanctimonious

311. Even after the rain began, Latisha continued to push forward and finish the marathon. Latisha is a _____ person.

312. Though the hurricane was approaching, the surfers thought it would be a great time to go surfing regardless of the risk. The surfers are being _____.

313. When friends came to play, Rachel would only let them play the games she selected; she even dictated where her friends would sit and what they could eat. Rachel is being _____.

314. At work, Tom boasted that he and his family never missed church on Sunday mornings; he did not mention that they always left services without saying hello to any of their friends or neighbors. Tom's boastful statements are _____.

315. Having already won two awards, the movie director coolly and calmly walked up to the podium to collect his third award of the evening. The director's manner is very _____.

316. Chang has been sulking in her room after learning she wasn't accepted by the college of her choice. She is even saying that she may not go to college at all. Chang is feeling _____.

317. Tom shocked the jurors when he stuck his tongue out at the judge during the court proceedings. Tom is being _____ toward the judge.

318. Reynaldo was a popular guest at dinner parties because of his ability to turn a phrase and to make funny, witty remarks. Reynaldo is very _____.

319. Though she was only an office assistant, Adele marched boldly into the vice president's office and calmly told him she would someday be his boss. Adele is being _____.

320. The teenage girls were jumping up and down in the aisles as their favorite band took the stage. The girls are acting in a(n) _____ manner.

Answers

301. To be *complaisant* is to comply with others and be willing to do what pleases others.

302. To be *apathetic* is to show a lack of interest or concern; to be indifferent.

303. To be *peremptory* is to be dictatorial, not allowing contradiction, or putting an end to debate or action.

304. To be *officious* is to be meddlesome, bossy, and eagerly offering unwanted advice.

305. An *impassive* person does not show his or her feelings, emotions, or pain.

306. To be *impetuous* is to display sudden, forceful energy or emotion, especially without thought or consideration of consequences.

307. Someone who is *ascetic* practices self-denial and does not allow him or herself pleasures or luxuries.

308. Someone who is *adamant* is unyielding to requests, appeals, or reason.

309. To be *querulous* is to complain and be generally discontented.

310. Something or someone who is *vitriolic* is savagely hostile or bitter.

311. Someone who is *mettlesome* is courageous and high-spirited.

312. To be *insouciant* is to be unconcerned, carefree, and indifferent.

313. Someone who is *imperious* is overbearing, bossy; domineering.

314. To be *sanctimonious* is to be hypocritically pious or devout; excessively self-righteous.

315. To be *nonchalant* is to be indifferent or cool; not showing anxiety or excitement.

316. To be *morose* is to be gloomy, sullen, or melancholy.

317. To be *flippant* is to not show proper seriousness or to be disrespectful.

318. To be *facetious* is to be humorous and witty; cleverly amusing.

319. To be *audacious* is to be fearlessly or recklessly daring; bold.

320. To be *ebullient* is to be bubbling over with enthusiasm, exuberant.

17

Government and Politics

Do you prefer the chaos of *anarchy* or the control of an *authoritarian* government? Whether your party is Democrat, Republican, Green, Liberal, Conservative, Socialist, or Independent, you will find the 20 words in this chapter helpful in describing and understanding various conditions of government and politics. You can find the answers to each question in this section at the end of the chapter.

Word List

anarchy (′an·ăr·kee) *n.* 1. the complete absence of government or control resulting in lawlessness. 2. political disorder and confusion. *The days immediately following the revolution were marked by anarchy.*

authoritarian (ă·thor·i·′tair·i·ăn) *adj.* favoring complete, unquestioning obedience to authority as opposed to individual freedom. *The military maintains an authoritarian environment for its officers and soldiers alike.*

demagogue (′dem·ă·gawg) *n.* a leader who obtains power by appealing to people's feelings and prejudices rather than by reasoning. *Hitler was the most infamous demagogue of the twentieth century.*

disenfranchise (dis·en·′fran·chīz) *v.* to deprive of the rights of citizenship, especially the right to vote. *The independent monitors were at polling locations to ensure neither party tried to disenfranchise incoming voters.*

egalitarian (i·gal·i·′tair·i·ăn) *adj.* characterized by or affirming the principle of equal political, social, civil, and economic rights for all persons. *Hannah was moved by the candidate's egalitarian speech.*

enclave (′en·klayv) *n.* a distinct territory lying wholly within the boundaries of another, larger territory. *The country of Lesotho is an enclave of South Africa.*

hegemony (hi·′jem·ŏ·nee) *n.* predominant influence or leadership, especially of one government over others. *A military takeover in the impoverished country secured the hegemony of the Centrist Party in its bid for power.*

imperialism (im·′peer·i·ă·liz·ĕm) *n.* the policy of extending the rule or authority of a nation or empire by acquiring other territories or dependencies. *Great Britain embraced imperialism, acquiring so many territories that the sun never set on the British Empire.*

laissez-faire (les·ay·′fair) *adj.* hands-off policy; noninterference by the government in business and economic affairs. *I believe a more laissez-faire approach by management would make everyone more cooperative and productive.*

nullify (′nul·ĭ·fī) *v.* 1. to make null (without legal force), invalidate. 2. to counteract or neutralize the effect of. *The opponents wanted to nullify the bill before it became a law.*

oligarchy (′ol·ĭ·gahr·kee) *n.* form of government in which the power is in the hands of a select few. *The small governing body calls itself a democracy, but it is clearly an oligarchy.*

partisan ('pahr·ti·zăn) *n.* 1. a person fervently and often uncritically supporting a group or cause. 2. a guerilla, a member of an organized body of fighters who attack or harass an enemy. *The partisan lobby could not see the logic of the opposing senator's argument and did not understand how the proposed legislation would infringe upon basic constitutional rights.*

precept ('pree·sept) *n.* a rule establishing standards of conduct. *The headmaster reviewed the precepts of the school with the students.*

proscribe (proh·'skrīb) *v.* 1. to prohibit, forbid; to banish or outlaw. 2. to denounce or condemn. *The king proscribed the worship of idols in his kingdom.*

protocol ('proh·tŏ·kawl) *n.* 1. etiquette; ceremony or procedure with regard to people's rank or status. 2. a first copy of a treaty or document. *Jackson was fired for repeatedly refusing to follow protocol.*

proxy ('prok·see) *n.* 1. a person or agent authorized to represent or act for another. 2. a document authorizing this substitution. *The president appointed a proxy to handle business matters during his absence.*

quid pro quo (kwid proh 'kwoh) *n.* a thing given in return for something; an equal exchange or substitution. *Let's come up with a quid pro quo arrangement that will create a win-win situation for both sides.*

reactionary (ree·'ak·shŏ·ner·ee) *n.* a person who favors political conservativism; one who is opposed to progress or liberalism. *It should be an interesting marriage: he's a reactionary and she's as liberal as they come.*

tendentious (ten·'den·shŭs) *adj.* biased, not impartial, partisan; supporting a particular cause or position. *The tendentious proposal caused an uproar on the Senate floor.*

totalitarian (toh·tal·i·'tair·i·ăn) *adj.* of a form of government in which those in control neither recognize nor tolerate rival parties or loyalties; demanding total submission of the individual to the needs of the state. *The totalitarian regime fell quickly when the people revolted.*

For numbers 321–330, read the following descriptions carefully. Decide which word best describes what is being said and circle the letter of the correct answer. (If you do not own this book, please write your answers on a separate piece of paper.)

321. A government that requires complete, unquestioning obedience to authority is
  a. authoritarian.
  b. laissez-faire.
  c. partisan.
  d. reactionary.

322. A government that holds power in the hands of a select few is a(n)
  a. proxy.
  b. hegemony.
  c. anarchy.
  d. oligarchy.

323. Someone who holds a firm or perhaps blind commitment to a cause or party is a(n)
  a. precept.
  b. partisan.
  c. enclave.
  d. proxy.

324. A political candidate who believes in the principles of equal political, social, civil, and economic rights for all would be referred to as
  a. laissez-faire.
  b. totalitarian.
  c. egalitarian.
  d. tendentious.

325. An individual who is authorized to represent, speak, or act for another is referred to as a
  a. proxy.
  b. precept.
  c. partisan.
  d. protocol.

326. When one political party dominates over another, it is referred to as
a. hegemony.
b. protocol.
c. anarchy.
d. quid pro quo.

327. A leader who appeals to people's feelings and prejudices rather than their sense of reason is a(n)
a. enclave.
b. demagogue.
c. reactionary.
d. oligarchy.

328. An independent country whose borders are completely surrounded by another country is referred to as a(n)
a. proxy.
b. protocol.
c. enclave.
d. precept.

329. Something that is biased and not impartial is referred to as
a. tendentious.
b. totalitarian.
c. authoritarian.
d. egalitarian.

330. The practice of expanding an empire by acquiring other dependencies or territories is known as
a. quid pro quo.
b. oligarchy.
c. imperialism.
d. anarchy.

For numbers 331–340, circle the answer that provides the best definition for each vocabulary word. (If you do not own this book, please
write your answers on a separate piece of paper.)

331. totalitarian
 a. government that encourages openness and freedom of
 expression
 b. government that demands total submission of the individual to
 the needs of the state
 c. government that encourages equal political, social, civil, and
 economic rights for all
 d. government that is comprised of freely elected representatives

332. laissez-faire
 a. government that practices noninterference in business/
 economic affairs
 b. government that practices state control over business/economic
 affairs
 c. government that practices principles embraced in France
 d. government that practices moderate control over business/
 economic affairs

333. anarchy
 a. complete absence of government or control resulting in
 lawlessness
 b. strict control over a country and its people by governmental
 authorities
 c. government that practices noninterference in business and
 economic affairs
 d. government that encourages equal political, social, civil, and
 economic rights for all

334. precept
 a. an official at a judicial hearing
 b. a voting irregularity
 c. a form of government that is represented by freely elected
 representatives
 d. a rule or principle establishing standards of conduct

335. reactionary
    a. a political conservative who opposes liberalism and/or progress
    b. a political liberal who opposes traditional and/or conservative leadership
    c. a professional protestor
    d. a professional lobbyist

336. proscribe
    a. to request in the form of a written document
    b. to prohibit, forbid, banish, or outlaw
    c. to vote in a secret legislative session
    d. to stall a legislative vote

337. protocol
    a. a political liberal
    b. a vote during a legislative session
    c. a ceremony or procedure regarding people's rank/status
    d. an illegal act of Congress

338. nullify
    a. to validate
    b. to invalidate
    c. to elevate in standing
    d. to confirm voting results

339. quid pro quo
    a. to stop legislative action through the courts
    b. to covertly meet with an opposition party
    c. to give something in return for something of similar value
    d. to acknowledge defeat

340. disenfranchise
    a. to embrace into a political system
    b. to deprive the rights of citizenship, especially the right to vote
    c. to break apart from an established political party
    d. to vote exclusively for one party's candidates

Answers

321. **a.** An *authoritarian* government favors complete, unquestioning obedience to authority as opposed to individual freedom.

322. **d.** An *oligarchy* is a government in which the power is in the hands of a select few.

323. **b.** A *partisan* is a person who fervently and often uncritically supports a group or cause.

324. **c.** To be *egalitarian* is to affirm the principles of equal political, social, civil, and economic rights for all persons.

325. **a.** A *proxy* is a person or agent authorized to represent or act for another.

326. **a.** *Hegemony* is when there is predominant influence or leadership, especially of one government over others.

327. **b.** A *demagogue* is a leader who obtains power by appealing to people's feelings and prejudices.

328. **c.** An *enclave* is a distinct territory lying wholly within the boundaries of another, larger territory.

329. **a.** To be *tendentious* is to be biased, not impartial; partisan.

330. **c.** *Imperialism* refers to the policy of extending the rule or authority of a nation or empire by acquiring other territories or dependencies.

331. **b.** A *totalitarian* government is one where those in control neither recognize nor tolerate rival parties or loyalties; they demand total submission of the individual to the needs of the state.

332. **a.** *Laissez-faire* is the practice by a government of letting its country's economic and business affairs function without government interference or oversight.

333. **a.** *Anarchy* refers to a situation where there has been a complete breakdown of governmental and/or legal authority resulting in chaos.

334. **d.** A *precept* is a rule that establishes certain standards of behavior or conduct.

335. **a.** A *reactionary* is someone who favors political conservatism and opposes liberal ideals and agendas.

336. **b.** If something is *proscribed*, it has been forbidden, outlawed, or banished.

337. **c.** *Protocol* refers to a form of etiquette or ceremonial procedures surrounding someone's rank or status.

338. **b.** To *nullify* something is to counteract it or make it invalid.

339. **c.** A *quid pro quo* is an arrangement where something is given in return for something of similar value.

340. **b.** To *disenfranchise* is to deprive someone of the rights of citizenship.

18

Person, Place, or Thing? Nouns II

Have you ever received *accolades* for a job well done or enjoyed the *catharsis* of a good tear-jerker? The 20 nouns in this chapter describe more interesting things you may have, do, see, or experience. You can find the answers to each question in this section at the end of the chapter.

Word List

abeyance (ă·ˈbay·ăns) *n.* suspension, being temporarily suspended or set aside. *Construction of the highway is in abeyance until we get agency approval.*

accolade (ˈak·ŏ·layd) *n.* 1. praise or approval. 2. a ceremonial embrace in greeting. 3. a ceremonious tap on the shoulder with a sword to mark the conferring of knighthood. *He received accolades from his superiors for finding ways to cut costs and increase productivity.*

accretion (ă·ˈkree·shŏn) *n.* 1. growth or increase by gradual, successive addition; building up. 2. (in biology) the growing together of parts that are normally separate. *The accretion of sediment in the harbor channel caused boats to run aground.*

alacrity (ă·ˈlak·ri·tee) *n.* a cheerful willingness; being happily ready and eager. *The alacrity she brought to her job helped her move up the corporate ladder quickly.*

asperity (ă·ˈsper·i·tee) *n.* harshness, severity; roughness of manner, ill temper, irritability. *The asperity that Marvin, the grumpy accountant, brought to the weekly meetings usually resulted in an early adjournment.*

catharsis (kă·ˈthahr·sis) *n.* the act of ridding or cleansing; relieving emotions via the experiences of others, especially through art. *Survivors of war often experience a catharsis when viewing Picasso's painting* Guernica, *which depicts the bombing of a town during the Spanish civil war.*

consternation (kon·stĕr·ˈnay·shŏn) *n.* a feeling of deep, incapacitating horror or dismay. *The look of consternation on the faces of the students taking the history exam alarmed the teacher, who thought he had prepared his students for the test.*

decorum (di·ˈkohr·ŭm) *n.* appropriateness of behavior, propriety; decency in manners and conduct. *When questions concerning decorum arise, I always refer to Emily Post, the etiquette guru.*

effrontery (i·ˈfrun·tĕ·ree) *n.* brazen boldness, impudence, insolence. *The customs officials were infuriated by the effrontery of the illegal alien who nonchalantly carried drugs into the country in his shirt pocket.*

eulogy (ˈyoo·lŏ·gee) *n.* a formal speech or piece of writing in praise of someone or something. *Richard was asked to give a eulogy for his fallen comrade.*

forbearance (for·ˈbair·ăns) *n.* patience, willingness to wait, tolerance. *Gustaf dreaded the security check in the airport, but he faced it with great forbearance because he knew it was for his own safety.*

guffaw (gu·'faw) *n.* a noisy, coarse burst of laughter. *Michael let out quite a guffaw when Jamal told him the outlandish joke.*

imbroglio (im·'brohl·yoh) *n.* a confused or difficult situation, usually involving disagreement. *An imbroglio developed when the bus drivers went on, leaving thousands of commuters stranded at the bus station with no way to get home.*

minutiae (mi·'noo·shi·ee) *n., pl.* very small details; trivial or trifling matters. *His attention to the minutiae of the process enabled him to make his great discovery.*

penury ('pen·yŭ·ree) *n.* extreme poverty, destitution. *After ten years of penury, it's good to be financially secure again.*

rigmarole ('rig·mă·rohl) (also *rigamarole*) *n.* 1. rambling, confusing, or incoherent talk. 2. a complicated, petty procedure. *We had to go through a great deal of rigmarole to get this approved.*

rubric ('roo·brik) *n.* 1. a class or category. 2. a heading, title, or note of explanation or direction. *I would put calculus under the rubric of college mathematics, not high school.*

savoir faire ('sav·wahr 'fair) *n.* knowledge of the right thing to do or say in a social situation; graceful tact. *Savoir faire is essential if you want to be a successful diplomat.*

umbrage ('um·brij) *n.* offense, resentment. *I took great umbrage at your suggestion that I twisted the truth.*

verisimilitude (ver·i·si·'mil·i·tood) *n.* the appearance of being true or real. *The movie aims for complete verisimilitude and has painstakingly recreated the details of everyday life in the 1920s.*

For questions 341–350, choose the best <u>synonym</u> for each vocabulary word. Circle the letter of the correct answer. (If you do not own this book, please write your answers on a separate piece of paper.)

341. abeyance
   a. obedience
   b. reluctance
   c. suspension
   d. relief

342. accolade
   a. praise
   b. disbelief
   c. impression
   d. happiness

343. accretion
   a. deletion
   b. agreement
   c. suspense
   d. accumulation

344. alacrity
   a. sadness
   b. eagerness
   c. bitterness
   d. loneliness

345. consternation
   a. dismay
   b. constellation
   c. reservation
   d. disbelief

346. forbearance
   a. poverty
   b. strength
   c. patience
   d. ancestry

347. minutiae
   a. microcosm
   b. regiment
   c. details
   d. pattern

348. penury
   a. destitution
   b. punishment
   c. judgment
   d. agony

349. umbrage
   a. protection
   b. offense
   c. transition
   d. gathering

350. verisimilitude
   a. deceit
   b. fanaticism
   c. similarity
   d. realism

For numbers 351–360, choose the word from the list below that best completes the sentence. Each word is used only once. Write your answer in the blank. (If you do not own this book, please write your answers on a separate piece of paper.)

asperity	guffaw
catharsis	imbroglio
decorum	rigmarole
effrontery	rubric
eulogy	savoir faire

351. No matter how many times I see *Madame Butterfly*, I always experience a(n) _____ because the opera is such a powerful and moving tragedy.

352. The essay was graded using a specific _____ with categories that a writer needed to address.

353. The young boy composed a(n) _____ for his recently departed grandmother that he planned to read at her memorial service.

354. I am always impressed by Hudson's _____; no matter what the situation, he always says the right thing.

355. Waterford's _____ in trying to take credit for Vanessa's work eventually got him fired.

356. Vanya, who once had the manners of a boor, now behaves with the utmost _____, thanks to etiquette lessons from his Aunt Sasha.

357. Anuj angered everyone in the audience when he let out a great _____ during the violin solo.

358. Ena's voice was full of _____ when she talked about the delays, lost luggage, and overbooking during her last trip abroad.

359. After Carter's surgery, he had to go through the _____ of filling out a myriad of insurance forms.

360. In the play, Rosalind causes a great _____ when she disguises herself as a man and another woman falls in love with her.

Answers

341. **c.** *Abeyance* means suspension or being temporarily suspended or set aside.

342. **a.** *Accolade* means praise or approval. It also means a ceremonial embrace in greeting or a ceremonial tap on the shoulder to confer knighthood.

343. **d.** *Accretion* is growth or increase by gradual, successive addition; building up.

344. **b.** *Alacrity* is cheerful willingness; being happily ready and eager.

345. **a.** *Consternation* is a feeling of deep, incapacitating horror or dismay.

346. **c.** *Forbearance* means patience; willingness to wait, tolerance.

347. **c.** *Minutiae* are very small details or trivial matters.

348. **a.** *Penury* means extreme poverty; destitution.

349. **b.** *Umbrage* means offense or resentment.

350. **d.** *Verisimilitude* is the appearance of being true or real.

351. *Catharsis* is the act of ridding or cleansing; relieving emotions via the experiences of others, especially through art.

352. A *rubric* is a class or category. It also means a heading, title, or note of explanation.

353. A *eulogy* is a formal speech or piece of writing in praise of someone or something.

354. *Savoir faire* is knowledge of the right thing to do or say in a social situation; graceful tact.

355. *Effrontery* means brazen boldness; impudence, insolence.

356. *Decorum* is appropriateness of behavior; decency in manners and conduct.

357. A *guffaw* is a noisy, coarse burst of laughter.

358. *Asperity* means harshness, severity; roughness of manner; ill temper or irritability.

359. *Rigmarole* means a complicated, petty procedure.

360. An *imbroglio* is a confused or difficult situation, usually involving disagreement.

19

What's It Like? More Words to Describe Things

Have you ever had a *harrowing* experience, such as a turbulent airplane ride? Have you ever paid an *exorbitant* price for dinner at a fancy restaurant? In this chapter, you will find 20 more words that will help you in your everyday life to describe, well . . . your everyday life. You can find the answers to each question in this section at the end of the chapter.

Word List

arcane (ahr·'kayn) *adj.* mysterious, secret, beyond comprehension. *A number of college students in the 1980s became involved in the arcane game known as "Dungeons and Dragons."*

blatant ('blay·tant) *adj.* completely obvious, not attempting to conceal in any way. *Samuel's blatant disregard of the rules earned him a two-week suspension.*

empirical (em·'pir·i·kal) *adj.* based on observation or experience rather than theory. *Frank's empirical data suggested that mice would climb over the walls of the maze to get to the cheese rather than navigate the maze itself.*

endemic (en·'dem·ik) *adj.* 1. prevalent in or characteristic of a specific area or group of people. 2. native to a particular region. *Kudzu, a hairy, purple-flowered vine thought to be endemic to the southeastern United States, was actually imported from Japan.*

exigent ('ek·si·jĕnt) *adj.* 1. urgent, requiring immediate action or attention; critical. 2. requiring much effort or precision, demanding. *The late-night call on Paul's cell phone concerned matters of an exigent nature.*

exorbitant (ig·'zor·bi·tănt) *adj.* greatly exceeding the bounds of what is normal or reasonable; inordinate and excessive. *Three thousand dollars is an exorbitant amount of money to pay for a scarf.*

expedient (ik·'spee·di·ĕnt) *adj.* 1. appropriate for a purpose, a suitable means to an end. 2. serving to promote one's own interests rather than principle. *A quick divorce was an expedient end to the couple's two-month marriage.*

fulsome ('fuul·sŏm) *adj.* offensive due to excessiveness, especially excess flattery or praise. *Her new coworker's fulsome attention bothered Kathryn.*

harrowing ('har·oh·ing) *adj.* distressing, creating great stress or torment. *The turbulent flight proved to be a harrowing experience for Jane.*

ineluctable (in·i·'luk·tă·bĕl) *adj.* certain, inevitable; not to be avoided or overcome. *The ineluctable outcome of the two-person race was that there would be one winner and one loser.*

inveterate (in·'vet·ĕ·rit) *adj.* habitual; deep rooted, firmly established. *I am an inveterate pacifist and unlikely to change my mind.*

multifarious (mul·ti·'fair·i·ŭs) *adj.* occuring in great variety, diversified; having many aspects. *The job requires the ability to handle multifarious tasks.*

pernicious (pĕr·'nish·ŭs) *adj.* deadly, harmful; very destructive. *Nancy's opponent started a pernicious rumor that destroyed her chances of winning.*

plaintive ('playn·tiv) *adj.* expressing sorrow; mournful, melancholy. *Janice's plaintive voice made me decide to stay and comfort her longer.*

resonant ('rez·ŏ·nănt) *adj.* echoing, resounding. *The new announcer at the stadium has a wonderfully resonant voice.*

stringent ('strin·jĕnt) *adj.* very strict; according to very rigorous rules, requirements, or standards. *The stringent eligibility requirements greatly limited the number of candidates for the scholarship.*

subliminal (sub·'lim·ĭ·năl) *adj.* below the threshold of consciousness. *Subliminal advertising is devious but effective.*

sundry ('sun·dree) *adj.* various, miscellaneous. *The sundry items in her backpack reveal a great deal about her personality.*

trenchant ('tren·chănt) *adj.* 1. penetrating, forceful; effective. 2. extremely perceptive, incisive. 3. clear-cut, sharply defined. *It was a trenchant argument, and it forced me to change my mind about the issue.*

tumultuous (too·'mul·choo·ŭs) *adj.* 1. creating an uproar; disorderly, noisy. 2. a state of confusion, turbulence, or agitation; tumult. *It was another tumultuous day for the stock market, and fluctuating prices wreaked havoc for investors.*

For numbers 361–380, circle the answer that best completes the prompt. (If you do not own this book, please write your answers on a separate piece of paper.)

361. A *multifarious* task would
    a. have many different components.
    b. have very few components.
    c. be very complex.
    d. be impossible to complete.

362. *Plaintive* cries would be
    a. musical, soothing.
    b. plain, uninteresting.
    c. loud, jarring.
    d. sorrowful, mournful.

363. People with *inveterate* beliefs
    a. can be easily manipulated.
    b. have adopted their beliefs from another.
    c. hold their beliefs deeply and passionately.
    d. change their beliefs frequently.

364. A prosecutor's *trenchant* closing statement would be
    a. a very effective closing statement.
    b. a very offensive closing statement.
    c. a very weak closing statement.
    d. a very confusing closing statement.

365. A *harrowing* experience is
    a. mundane and boring.
    b. distressing and upsetting.
    c. sensual and romantic.
    d. happy and joyful.

366. An item of clothing that is *exorbitant* in price is
    a. extremely inexpensive.
    b. extremely expensive.
    c. on sale.
    d. a good value.

367. An *arcane* organization is one that
   a. actively recruits new members.
   b. is very old and outdated.
   c. is very secretive and mysterious.
   d. is located in a foreign land.

368. A *pernicious* virus would be
   a. acquired in the sub-Saharan desert.
   b. deadly and very destructive.
   c. contagious and easily transmitted.
   d. mild and easily treated.

369. A *blatant* statement is
   a. obvious.
   b. secretive.
   c. fabricated.
   d. loud.

370. *Empirical* data is data that
   a. has been acquired through a detailed study of relevant text.
   b. has been acquired from ancient empires.
   c. has been gathered through observation and/or experience.
   d. has been proven false.

371. "Corn is *endemic* to South America" means
   a. corn was introduced to South America by European settlers.
   b. corn is a native plant of South America.
   c. corn caused an epidemic in South America.
   d. corn is imported into South America.

372. If a boarding school has *stringent* rules, the rules will be
   a. contemporary and forward thinking.
   b. outdated and antiquated.
   c. loose and liberal.
   d. strict and rigorous.

373. An *ineluctable* consequence
   a. cannot be avoided.
   b. is not desirable.
   c. would not be anticipated.
   d. can be avoided.

374. A *subliminal* message
  a. is easy to identify.
  b. originates from another country.
  c. is received at the subconscious level.
  d. is written in secret code.

375. A *resonant* sound
  a. echoes through a space.
  b. is harsh and piercing.
  c. is soft and delicate.
  d. cannot be heard by humans.

376. An *expedient* resolution is
  a. slow and cumbersome.
  b. inappropriate for the situation.
  c. quick and fast-acting.
  d. appropriate for the situation.

377. An *exigent* medical condition would
  a. affect the extremities.
  b. be slow to develop.
  c. be commonplace and of little concern.
  d. require immediate attention.

378. Stores that sell *sundry* items
  a. sell items appropriate for long journeys in the sun.
  b. sell items expressly for farming and ranching.
  c. sell an array of miscellaneous items.
  d. sell only food-stuffs.

379. If your boss believes you to be *fulsome*, you are probably
  a. offending your boss by offering him or her excessive praise.
  b. irritating your boss by being lazy and uncooperative.
  c. pleasing your boss by being an exemplary employee.
  d. inspiring your boss by being courageous and bold.

380. A *tumultuous* crowd at a sporting event would be
  a. very rowdy and disorderly.
  b. very respectful and honorable.
  c. very quiet and indifferent.
  d. very loyal and dedicated.

Answers

361. **a.** *Multifarious* means having many different aspects or components.

362. **d.** *Plaintive* means expressing sorrow; mournful, melancholy.

363. **c.** *Inveterate* beliefs are deep-rooted or firmly established.

364. **a.** A *trenchant* argument is effective, penetrating, or forceful.

365. **b.** A *harrowing* experience is distressing and creates great torment.

366. **b.** An *exorbitant* price greatly exceeds the bounds of normalcy.

367. **c.** An *arcane* organization is secretive and mysterious.

368. **b.** *Pernicious* means deadly and destructive.

369. **a.** *Blatant* means completely obvious and not concealed.

370. **c.** *Empirical* means based on observation and experience rather than theory.

371. **b.** *Endemic* means characteristic of or native to a specific area or culture.

372. **d.** *Stringent* means very strict.

373. **a.** *Ineluctable* consequences are certain and unavoidable.

374. **c.** *Subliminal* messages are beyond the threshold of consciousness.

375. **a.** A *resonant* sound echoes through a space.

376. **d.** *Expedient* means correct or appropriate for the situation.

377. **d.** An *exigent* situation requires immediate attention.

378. **c.** *Sundry* means a wide array, or miscellaneous.

379. **a.** To be *fulsome* is to offend due to excessiveness especially with flattery or praise.

380. **a.** *Tumultuous* crowds are disorderly and noisy.

20

Word Pairs IV

Do you tend to be *taciturn*, or are you the talkative type? Are you *shiftless* on a hot summer afternoon, or are you always checking things off from your "to do" list? This is the final chapter of *word pairs*—pairs of words that are almost exactly the same in meaning. Each word pair chapter contains ten sets of synonyms. You can find the answers to each question in this section at the end of the chapter.

Word List

abjure (ab·ˈjoor) *v.* 1. to repudiate, renounce under oath. 2. to give up or reject. *When Joseph became a citizen, he had to abjure his allegiance to his country of origin.*

conundrum (kŏ·ˈnun·drŭm) *n.* a hard riddle, enigma; a puzzling question or problem. *Michelle's logic professor gave the class a conundrum to work on over the weekend.*

enigma (ĕ·ˈnig·mă) *n.* 1. something that is puzzling or difficult to understand; a perplexing occurrence or thing that cannot be explained. 2. a baffling problem or difficult riddle. *How Winston came to be the president of this organization is a true enigma.*

equivocate (i·ˈkwiv·ŏ·kayt) *v.* to use unclear or ambiguous language in order to mislead or conceal the truth. *Raj tried to equivocate when explaining why he came home after his curfew.*

haughty (ˈhaw·tee) *adj.* scornfully arrogant and condescending; acting as though one is superior and others unworthy; disdainful. *Stanley is so often haughty that he has very few friends.*

indolent (ˈin·dŏ·lĕnt) *adj.* 1. lazy, lethargic; inclined to avoid labor. 2. causing little or no pain; slow to grow or heal. *Iris's indolent attitude did not bode well for her professional future.*

iota (ī·ˈoh·tă) *n.* a very small amount; the smallest possible quantity. *Professor Carlton is unpopular because he doesn't have one iota of respect for his students.*

obstreperous (ob·ˈstrep·ĕ·rŭs) *adj.* noisily and stubbornly defiant; aggressively boisterous, unruly. *The obstreperous child refused to go to bed.*

obtrusive (ŏb·ˈtroo·siv) *adj.* 1. prominent, undesirably noticeable. 2. projecting, thrusting out. 3. tending to push one's self or one's ideas upon others; forward, intrusive. *Thankfully, Minsun survived the accident, but she was left with several obtrusive scars.*

pertinacious (pur·tĭ·ˈnay·shŭs) *adj.* extremely stubborn or persistent; holding firmly to a belief, purpose, or course of action. *The pertinacious journalist finally uncovered the truth about the factory's illegal disposal of toxins.*

prevaricate (pri·ˈvar·ĭ·kayt) *v.* to tell lies; to stray from or evade the truth. *Quit prevaricating and tell me what really happened.*

repudiate (ri·ˈpyoo·di·ayt) *v.* to disown, disavow; reject completely. *Mrs. Tallon has repeatedly repudiated your accusations.*

reticent ('ret·i·sĕnt) *adj.* tending to keep one's thoughts and feelings to oneself; reserved, untalkative; silent. *Annette is very reticent, so don't expect her to tell you much about herself.*

salient ('say·li·ĕnt) *adj.* 1. conspicuous, prominent, highly noticeable; drawing attention through a striking quality. 2. moving by leaps or springs; jutting out. *Siobhán's most salient feature is her stunning auburn hair.*

scintilla (sin·'til·ă) *n.* a trace or particle; minute amount, iota. *She has not one scintilla of doubt about his guilt.*

shiftless ('shift·lis) *adj.* lazy and inefficient; lacking ambition, initiative, or purpose. *My shiftless roommate has failed all of his classes.*

supercilious (soo·pĕr·'sil·i·ŭs) *adj.* haughty, scornful, disdainful. *Sunil's supercilious attitude and sarcastic remarks annoy me greatly.*

taciturn ('tas·i·turn) *adj.* habitually untalkative, reserved. *I've always known him to be taciturn, but yesterday he regaled me with tales of his hiking adventures.*

tenacious (tĕ·'nay·shŭs) *adj.* 1. holding firmly to something, such as a right or principle; persistent, stubbornly unyielding. 2. holding firmly, cohesive. 3. sticking firmly, adhesive. 4. (of memory) retentive. *When it comes to fighting for equality, she is the most tenacious person I know.*

truculent ('truk·yŭ·lĕnt) *adj.* 1. defiantly aggressive; 2. fierce, violent. 3. bitterly expressing opposition. *The outspoken congresswoman gave a truculent speech arguing against the proposal.*

Crossword Puzzle Directions

In this puzzle, there is one clue for each set of synonyms, so each clue is offered twice. Read the definition provided in the clue and determine which two words share that meaning. Then determine which of those synonyms fits the designated crossword squares.

Word Pairs IV Crossword Puzzle

ACROSS

383. renounce, reject completely (paired with 382 down)

390. stubbornly defiant or aggressive; fiercely unruly, violent (paired with 393 across)

393. stubbornly defiant or aggressive; fiercely unruly, violent (paired with 390 across)

395. very small amount (paired with 392 down)

396. lazy, lacking ambition (paired with 389 down)

398. untalkative, reserved (paired with 400 across)

400. untalkative, reserved (paired with 398 across)

DOWN

381. scornfully condescending, disdainful (paired with 397 down)

382. renounce, reject completely (paired with 383 across)

384. speak falsely; use unclear language to hide the truth (paired with 391 down)

385. prominent, highly noticeable; projecting out (paired with 394 down)

386. baffling riddle; puzzling question or problem (paired with 399 down)

387. holding firmly, as to a belief; extremely stubborn or persistent (paired with 388 down)

388. holding firmly, as to a belief; extremely stubborn or persistent (paired with 387 down)

389. lazy, lacking ambition (paired with 396 across)

391. speak falsely; use unclear language to hide the truth (paired with 384 down)

392. very small amount (paired with 395 across)

394. prominent, highly noticeable; projecting out (paired with 385 down)

397. scornfully condescending, disdainful (paired with 381 down)

399. baffling riddle; puzzling question or problem (paired with 386 down)

Answers

The following words are *word pairs*:

abjure, repudiate
conundrum, enigma
equivocate, prevaricate
haughty, supercilious
indolent, shiftless
iota, scintilla
obstreperous, truculent
obtrusive, salient
pertinacious, tenacious
reticent, taciturn

Across
383. To *abjure* means to *repudiate*, renounce under oath; to give up, reject.

390. *Obstreperous* means noisily and stubbornly defiant; aggressively boisterous, unruly; *truculent*.

393. *Truculent* means defiantly aggressive, *obstreperous*; fierce, violent; bitterly expressing opposition.

395. An *iota* is a very small amount, a *scintilla*; the smallest possible quantity.

396. *Shiftless* means lazy and inefficient, *indolent*; lacking ambition, initiative, or purpose.

398. *Reticent* means tending to keep one's thoughts and feelings to oneself; reserved, untalkative, *taciturn*.

400. *Taciturn* means habitually untalkative, reserved; *reticent*.

Down
381. *Supercilious* means *haughty*; scornful, disdainful.

382. To *repudiate* means to disown; disavow, reject completely, *abjure*.

384. To *equivocate* means to use unclear or ambiguous language in order to mislead or conceal the truth; *prevaricate*.

385. *Obtrusive* means prominent, undesirably noticeable; projecting, thrusting out; *salient*. It also means tending to push one's self or ideas upon others; intrusive.

386. A *conundrum* is a hard riddle, an *enigma*; a puzzling question or problem.

387. *Pertinacious* means extremely stubborn or persistent; holding firmly to a belief, purpose, or course of action; *tenacious*.

388. *Tenacious* means holding firmly to something such as a belief; stubbornly unyielding, *pertinacious*. It also means cohesive, sticking firmly, adhesive; of memory, retentive.

389. *Indolent* means lazy; lethargic, inclined to avoid labor, *shiftless*. It also means causing little or no pain; slow to grow or heal.

391. To *prevaricate* means to tell lies, to stray from or evade the truth; to *equivocate*.

392. A *scintilla* is a trace or particle, minute amount; *iota*.

394. *Salient* means conspicuous, prominent, highly noticeable, *obtrusive*; drawing attention through a striking quality; jutting out.

397. *Haughty* means scornfully arrogant and condescending; acting as though one is superior; disdainful, *supercilious*.

399. An *enigma* is something that is puzzling or difficult to understand; a perplexing, inexplicable thing; a baffling problem or difficult riddle; *conundrum*.

381 SUPERCILIOUS
382 REPUDIATE
383 ABJURE
384 EQUIVOCATE
385 OBTRUSIVE
386 CONUNDRUM
387 PERTINACIOUS
388 TENACIOUS
389 INDOLENT
390 OBSTREPEROUS
391 PREVARICATE
392 SCINTILLA
393 TRUCULENT
394 SALIENT
395 IOTA
396 SHIFTLESS
397 HAUGHTY
398 RETICENT
399 ENIGMA
400 TACITURN

21

Love and Hate, War and Peace

Are you a *contentious* person, or do you try to avoid confrontation? Do you remember the *ardor* you felt towards your first true love? The 20 words in this chapter are about our two most basic emotions, love and hate, and the two basic states of human relationships, war and peace. You can find the answers to each question in this section at the end of the chapter.

Word List

abhor (ab·ʹhohr) *v.* to regard with horror, detest. *I abhor such hypocrisy!*

aficionado (ă·fish·yŏ·ʹnah·doh) *n.* a fan or devotee, especially of a sport or pastime. *The Jefferson's attendance at every game proved that they were true aficionados of baseball.*

altercation (awl·tĕr·ʹkay·shŏn) *n.* a heated dispute or quarrel. *To prevent an altercation at social functions, one should avoid discussing politics and religion.*

apocalypse (ă·ʹpok·ă·lips) *n.* a cataclysmic event bringing about total devastation or the end of the world. *Many people feared an apocalypse would immediately follow the development of nuclear weapons.*

ardor (ʹahr·dŏr) *n.* fiery intensity of feeling; passionate enthusiasm, zeal. *The ardor Larry brought to the campaign made him a natural campaign spokesperson.*

bellicose (ʹbel·ĭ·kohs) *adj.* belligerent, quarrelsome, eager to wage war. *There was little hope for peace following the election of a candidate known for his bellicose nature.*

cabal (kă·ʹbal) *n.* 1. a scheme or conspiracy. 2. a small group joined in a secret plot. *With Antonio as their leader, the members of the unit readied themselves to begin the cabal.*

contentious (kŏn·ʹten·shŭs) *adj.* 1. quarrelsome, competitive, quick to fight. 2. controversial, causing contention. *With two contentious candidates on hand, it was sure to be a lively debate.*

fervent (ʹfur·vĕnt) *adj.* 1. having or showing great emotion; ardent, zealous 2. extremely hot, burning. *Norman had a fervent belief that aliens had already landed on earth.*

fervor (ʹfur·vŏr) *n.* zeal, ardor; intense emotion. *The fervor of the fans in the stands helped propel the team to victory.*

incursion (in·ʹkur·zhŏn) *n.* a raid or temporary invasion of someone else's territory; the act of entering or running into a territory or domain. *There was an incursion on the western border of their country.*

misanthrope (mis·ʹan·throhp) *n.* one who hates or distrusts humankind. *Pay no mind to his criticism; he's a real misanthrope, and no one can do anything right in his eyes.*

nemesis (ʹnem·ĕ·sis) *n.* 1. source of harm or ruin; the cause of one's misery or downfall; bane. 2. agent of retribution or vengeance. *In* Frankenstein, *the monster that Victor creates becomes his nemesis.*

odious (′oh·di·ŭs) *adj.* contemptible, hateful, detestable. *This is an odious policy that will only damage the environment more.*

penchant (′pen·chănt) *n.* a strong inclination or liking. *I have a real penchant for science fiction writing and spend hours reading my favorite authors every night.*

pillage (′pil·ij) *v.* to forcibly rob of goods, especially in time of war; to plunder. *The barbarians pillaged the village before destroying it with fire.*

placid (′plas·id) *adj.* calm and peaceful; free from disturbance or tumult. *Lake Placid is as calm and peaceful as its name suggests.*

rancor (′rang·kŏr) *n.* a bitter feeling of ill will; long-lasting resentment. *Greg is full of rancor towards his brother, and this causes tension at family gatherings.*

reprisal (ri·′prī·zăl) *n.* 1. an act of retaliation for an injury with the intent of inflicting at least as much harm in return. 2. the practice of using political or military force without actually resorting to war. *The president promised a swift reprisal for the attack.*

xenophobia (zen·ŏ·′foh·bi·ă) *n.* a strong dislike, distrust, or fear of foreigners. *Many atrocities have been committed because of xenophobia.*

For questions 401–410, read the sentences below carefully. Decide which vocabulary word best completes the sentence. Circle the letter of the correct answer. (If you do not own this book, please write your answers on a separate piece of paper.)

401. A person who owns dozens of Mozart CDs and repeatedly goes to performances of his music is a Mozart
   a. penchant.
   b. misanthrope.
   c. fervor.
   d. aficionado.

402. Something that is hateful or detestable is
   a. fervent.
   b. full of ardor.
   c. odious.
   d. an aficionado.

403. A person who seems to dislike and distrust everyone
   a. suffers from xenophobia.
   b. is a misanthrope.
   c. is full of rancor.
   d. is odious.

404. A person's passionate love for his or her spouse would be called
   a. ardor.
   b. rancor.
   c. xenophobia.
   d. odious.

405. If you detest or despise something, you
   a. are fervent.
   b. have a penchant for it.
   c. are a misanthrope.
   d. abhor it.

406. If you have a strong liking for something, you
   a. abhor it.
   b. have a penchant for it.
   c. feel rancor toward it.
   d. are a misanthrope.

407. If you feel intense passion or zeal for something, you
    a. abhor it.
    b. feel fervor.
    c. feel rancor.
    d. have a penchant for it.

408. A person who fears or dislikes foreigners
    a. suffers from xenophobia.
    b. is an aficionado.
    c. has a penchant for other countries.
    d. feels ardor towards foreigners.

409. If you feel a great deal of resentment or ill will towards someone, you feel
    a. ardor.
    b. odious.
    c. rancor.
    d. xenophobia.

410. A person who is intensely zealous and emotional about something
    a. is fervent about it.
    b. feels rancor.
    c. is odious.
    d. abhors it.

For questions 411–420, read the following sentences carefully. Decide which answer best describes the vocabulary word in the prompt. Circle the letter of the correct answer. (If you do not own this book, please write your answers on a separate piece of paper.)

411. If you were involved in an *altercation*, you
    a. had an accident.
    b. had a heated argument.
    c. served in a war.
    d. were part of a conspiracy.

412. If you are a *contentious* person, you
    a. are usually right.
    b. believe in "an eye for an eye."
    c. always try to keep the peace.
    d. are very competitive and quarrelsome.

413. If you are part of a *cabal*, you
   a. are involved in a secret plot.
   b. are participating in a protest.
   c. belong to the majority.
   d. are fighting against the enemy.

414. If you are a *bellicose* leader, you
   a. do everything in your power to avoid war.
   b. are eager to wage war.
   c. remain neutral during international conflicts.
   d. treat all citizens equally.

415. If an *apocalypse* is near, you can expect
   a. a period of extended peace.
   b. a time of anarchy.
   c. total devastation and destruction.
   d. an invasion.

416. If your country suffers an *incursion*, your territory
   a. has been invaded.
   b. is in a depression.
   c. has seceded to form a new state.
   d. has had a natural disaster.

417. If you meet your *nemesis*, you meet
   a. the leader of your country.
   b. your guardian angel.
   c. the cause of your misfortunes.
   d. the person who decides your fate.

418. If you *pillage* a village, you
   a. set it on fire.
   b. destroy it with bombs.
   c. negotiate peace between warring tribes.
   d. ransack it and steal as much as you can.

419. If you are a *placid* person, you
  a. are usually calm and peaceful.
  b. are always trying to pick a fight.
  c. are disloyal.
  d. are not to be trusted.

420. If you plan a *reprisal*, you
  a. plan to surrender.
  b. plan to retaliate.
  c. hope to negotiate a cease-fire.
  d. plan to desert the army.

Answers

401.   **d.** An *aficionado* is a fan or devotee.

402.   **c.** Something *odious* is contemptible, hateful, or detestable.

403.   **b.** A *misanthrope* is someone who hates or distrusts humankind.

404.   **a.** *Ardor* is a fiery intensity of feeling; passionate enthusiasm, zeal.

405.   **d.** To *abhor* something is to regard it with horror; to detest it.

406.   **b.** A *penchant* is a strong inclination or liking.

407.   **b.** *Fervor* means zeal, ardor, or intense emotion.

408.   **a.** *Xenophobia* is a strong dislike, distrust, or fear of foreigners.

409.   **c.** *Rancor* is a bitter feeling of ill will; long-lasting resentment.

410.   **a.** *Fervent* means having or showing great emotion; ardent, zealous. It also means extremely hot, burning.

411.   **b.** An *altercation* is a heated dispute or quarrel.

412.   **d.** A *contentious* person is quarrelsome, competitive, quick to fight. *Contentious* also means controversial, causing contention.

413.   **a.** A *cabal* is a scheme or conspiracy; a small group joined in a secret plot.

414.   **b.** A *bellicose* person is belligerent, quarrelsome; eager to wage war.

415.   **c.** An *apocalypse* is a cataclysmic event that brings total devastation or the end of the world.

416.   **a.** An *incursion* is a raid or temporary invasion of someone else's territory.

417.   **c.** A *nemesis* is a source of harm or ruin; the cause of one's misery or downfall, bane; agent of retribution or vengeance.

418. **d.** To *pillage* means to forcibly rob of goods; to plunder.

419. **a.** *Placid* means calm and peaceful; free from disturbance.

420. **b.** A *reprisal* is an act of retaliation for an injury. It is also the practice of using political or military force without actually resorting to war.

22

Opposites Attract— Antonyms II

Are you *frugal* with your money, or do you tend to be *prodigal* and spend it extravagantly? The 20 words in this chapter include ten pairs of antonyms. You can find the answers to each question in this section at the end of the chapter.

Word List

acrid (ˈak·rid) *adj.* 1. having an unpleasantly bitter, sharp taste or smell. 2. bitter or caustic in language or manner. *The burning tires in the junkyard gave off an acrid odor.*

antithesis (an·ˈtith·ĕ·sis) *n.* the direct or exact opposite; opposition or contrast. *Martin's liberal parenting style is the antithesis of my conservative style.*

austere (aw·ˈsteer) *adj.* 1. severe or stern in attitude or appearance. 2. simple, unadorned, very plain. *With its simple but functional furniture and its obvious lack of decorative elements, the interior of the Shaker meeting hall was considered austere by many people.*

debacle (di·ˈbah·kĕl) *n.* 1. a sudden disaster or collapse; a total defeat or failure. 2. a sudden breaking up or breaking loose; violent flood waters, often caused by the breaking up of ice in a river. *Putting the bridge's supporting beams in loose sand caused a total debacle when the sand shifted and the bridge fell apart.*

éclat (ay·ˈklah) *n.* conspicuous success; great acclaim or applause; brilliant performance or achievement. *Even the ruinous deceit of the envious Salieri could not impede the dazzling éclat of the young and gifted Mozart.*

euphoria (yoo·ˈfohr·i·ă) *n.* a feeling of well-being or high spirits. *When falling in love, it is not uncommon to experience feelings of euphoria.*

frugal (ˈfroo·găl) *adj.* 1. careful and economical; sparing, thrifty. 2. costing little. *My grandparents survived the Great Depression by being very frugal.*

impecunious (im·pĕ·ˈkyoo·ni·ŭs) *adj.* having little or no money; poor, penniless. *Many impecunious immigrants in the United States eventually were able to make comfortable lives for themselves.*

intractable (in·ˈtrak·tă·bĕl) *adj.* unmanageable, unruly, stubborn. *The young colt was intractable, and training had to be cancelled temporarily.*

malaise (mă·ˈlayz) *n.* a feeling of illness or unease. *After his malaise persisted for more than a week, Nicholas went to see a doctor.*

meretricious (mer·ĕ·ˈtrish·ŭs) *adj.* gaudy, tawdry; showily attractive but false or insincere. *With its casinos and attractions, some people consider Las Vegas the most meretricious city in the country.*

opulent (ˈop·yŭ·lĕnt) *adj.* 1. possessing great wealth, affluent. 2. abundant, luxurious. *Lee is very wealthy, but he does not live an opulent lifestyle.*

paucity ('paw·si·tee) *n.* scarcity; smallness of supply or quantity. *The paucity of food in the area drove the herd farther and farther to the south.*

piquant ('pee·kănt) *adj.* 1. agreeably pungent; sharp or tart in taste. 2. pleasantly stimulating or provocative. *The spicy shrimp salad is wonderfully piquant.*

plethora ('pleth·ŏ·ră) *n.* an overabundance, extreme excess. *There was a plethora of food at the reception.*

prodigal ('prod·ĭ·găl) *adj.* 1. recklessly wasteful or extravagant, especially with money. 2. given in great abundance; lavish or profuse. *The parable of the prodigal son shows what can happen when money is wasted.*

profligate ('prof·lĭ·git) *adj.* 1. recklessly wasteful or extravagant; prodigal. 2. lacking moral restraint; dissolute. *The profligate man quickly depleted his fortune.*

propinquity (proh·'ping·kwi·tee) *n.* 1. proximity, nearness. 2. affinity, similarity in nature. *The two scientific elements demonstrate a remarkable propinquity.*

provident ('prov·i·dĕnt) *adj.* wisely providing for future needs; frugal, economical. *Because my parents were so provident, I didn't have to struggle to pay for college.*

tractable ('trak·tă·bĕl) *adj.* easily managed or controlled; obedient, docile. *In the novel* Brave New World, *the world controllers use hypnosis and a "happiness drug" to make everyone tractable.*

For questions 421–430, you will find the antonyms paired together in the form of an analogy. Choose the set of antonyms that best defines the two vocabulary words and completes the analogy. Circle the letter of the correct answer. (If you do not own this book, please write your answers on a separate piece of paper.)

421. acrid : piquant ::
  a. unpleasant : pleasant
  b. dry : wet
  c. stale : fresh
  d. heavy : light

422. paucity : plethora ::
  a. mighty : frail
  b. few : many
  c. bravery : cowardice
  d. sickness : health

423. meretricious : austere ::
  a. kind : wicked
  b. flexible : stubborn
  c. generous : stingy
  d. gaudy : plain

424. frugal : prodigal ::
  a. empty : full
  b. thrifty : wasteful
  c. hungry : satiated
  d. lazy : energetic

425. impecunious : opulent ::
  a. small : big
  b. wild : tame
  c. poor : rich
  d. beginning : end

426. antithesis : propinquity ::
  a. difference : similarity
  b. none : all
  c. disapproval : approval
  d. rejection : acceptance

427. debacle : éclat ::
  a. disagreement : agreement
  b. failure : success
  c. bias : objectivity
  d. radical : conservative

428. euphoria : malaise ::
  a. uncertainty : certainty
  b. acceptance : alienation
  c. happiness : misery
  d. journey : destination

429. intractable : tractable ::
  a. unmanageable : obedient
  b. incapable : capable
  c. far-fetched : plausible
  d. unusual : common

430. profligate : provident ::
  a. profit : debt
  b. ignorant : wise
  c. unlikely : likely
  d. extravagant : economical

For questions 431–440, choose the definition that is most nearly the *opposite* of the selected vocabulary word. The correct answer will be both the vocabulary word's *antonym* and the definition for another word from this chapter. (If you do not own this book, please write your answers on a separate piece of paper.)

431. intractable
  a. stubborn
  b. willing
  c. unbearable
  d. manageable

432. meretricious
  a. malicious
  b. unadorned
  c. incapable
  d. generous

433. prodigal
  a. wise
  b. expensive
  c. thrifty
  d. extravagant

434. impecunious
  a. uncontrollable
  b. wealthy
  c. reckless
  d. middle-class

435. debacle
  a. acclaim
  b. approval
  c. disappointment
  d. disaster

436. malaise
  a. uneasiness
  b. health
  c. youth
  d. reward

437. acrid
  a. frustrating
  b. very narrow
  c. agreeably sharp
  d. unpleasant, brusque

438. provident
  a. frugal
  b. wasteful
  c. future
  d. past

439. plethora
  a. scarcity
  b. greatness
  c. immensity
  d. brevity

440. propinquity
  a. unease
  b. purity
  c. nearness
  d. opposite

Answers

421. **a.** *Acrid* means having an unpleasantly bitter, sharp taste or smell; bitter or caustic in language or manner. *Piquant* means agreeably pungent, sharp or tart in taste; pleasantly stimulating or provocative.

422. **b.** *Paucity* means scarcity, smallness of supply or quantity. *Plethora* means an overabundance, extreme excess.

423. **d.** *Meretricious* means gaudy, tawdry, showily attractive but false or insincere. *Austere* means severe or stern in attitude or appearance; simple, unadorned, plain.

424. **b.** *Frugal* means careful and economical, sparing, thrifty. *Prodigal* means recklessly wasteful or extravagant, especially with money.

425. **c.** *Impecunious* means having little or no money; poor, penniless. *Opulent* means possessing great wealth; affluent.

426. **a.** *Antithesis* means the direct or exact opposite; contrast. *Propinquity* means proximity; affinity, similarity in nature.

427. **b.** A *debacle* is a sudden disaster or total failure. *Éclat* is conspicuous success, great acclaim, or brilliant achievement.

428. **c.** *Euphoria* is a feeling of well-being and high spirits. *Malaise* is a feeling of illness or unease.

429. **a.** *Intractable* means unmanageable, unruly, or stubborn. *Tractable* means easily managed or controlled; obedient, docile.

430. **d.** *Profligate* means recklessly wasteful or extravagant; prodigal, lacking moral restraint. *Provident* means wisely providing for future needs; frugal.

431. **d.** *Intractable* means unmanageable, unruly, or stubborn. Its antonym is *tractable*, which means easily managed or controlled; obedient, docile.

432. b. *Meretricious* means gaudy, tawdry, and showily attractive but false or insincere. Its antonym is *austere*, which means severe or stern in attitude or appearance; simple, unadorned, plain.

433. c. *Prodigal* means recklessly wasteful or extravagant, especially with money. Its antonym is *frugal*, which means careful and economical, sparing, thrifty.

434. b. *Impecunious* means having little or no money; poor, penniless. Its antonym is *opulent*, which means possessing great wealth, affluent.

435. a. A *debacle* is a sudden disaster or total failure. Its antonym is *éclat*, which means conspicuous success, great acclaim, or brilliant achievement.

436. b. *Malaise* is a feeling of illness or unease. Its antonym is *euphoria*, which is a feeling of well-being and high spirits.

437. c. *Acrid* means having an unpleasantly bitter, sharp taste or smell; bitter or caustic in language or manner. Its antonym is *piquant*, which means agreeably pungent, sharp, or tart in taste; pleasantly stimulating or provocative.

438. b. *Provident* means wisely providing for future needs; frugal. Its antonym is *profligate*, which means recklessly wasteful or extravagant; prodigal. It also means lacking moral restraint.

439. a. *Plethora* means an overabundance, extreme excess. Its antonym is *paucity*, which means scarcity, smallness of supply or quantity.

440. d. *Propinquity* means proximity; affinity, similarity in nature. Its antonym is *antithesis*, which means the direct or exact opposite; contrast.

23

Words about Religion and Words from Stories and Myths

Do you know anyone who is *mercurial* and often changes moods suddenly? Have you ever been the happy recipient of a *gargantuan* bonus? The 20 words in this chapter are common words about religion and sacred things that come from stories or ancient myths. You can find the answers to each question in this section at the end of the chapter.

Word List

apostate (ă·ˈpos·tayt) *n.* one who abandons long-held religious or political convictions. *Disillusioned with the religious life due to recent scandals in the church, Reverend Gift lost his faith and left the ministry, not caring if he'd be seen as an apostate by colleagues who chose to remain.*

apotheosis (ă·poth·i·ˈoh·sis) *n.* deification; an exalted or glorified ideal. *Lancelot was the apotheosis of chivalry until he met Guinivere.*

blasphemy (ˈblas·fĕ·mee) *n.* contemptuous or irreverent acts, utterances, attitudes, or writings against God or other things considered sacred; disrespect of something sacrosanct. *If you had committed blasphemy during the Inquisition, you would have been tortured and killed.*

desecrate (ˈdes·ĕ·krayt) *v.* to violate the sacredness of, to profane. *Someone desecrated the local cemetery by spray-painting graffiti on tombstones.*

dogma (ˈdawg·mă) *n.* a system of principles or beliefs; a prescribed doctrine. *Some find the dogma inherent in religion a comfort, whereas others find it too restrictive.*

draconian (dray·ˈkoh·ni·ăn) *adj.* very harsh, extremely severe (especially of a law or punishment). *Students of international policy are often shocked by the draconian punishments used by other countries for seemingly minor offences.*

gargantuan (gahr·ˈgan·choo·ăn) *adj.* gigantic, huge. *It was a gargantuan supermarket for such a small town.*

hallow (ˈhal·oh) *v.* to make holy, consecrate. *The religious leader proclaimed the new worship hall a hallowed space.*

imprecation (im·prĕ·ˈkay·shŏn) *n.* an invocation of evil, a curse. *In the book I'm reading, the gypsy queen levies an imprecation on the lead character.*

infidel (ˈin·fi·dĕl) *n.* 1. a person with no religious beliefs. 2. a non-believer; one who does not accept a particular religion, doctrine, or system of beliefs. *Because Tom had been raised with strict religious beliefs, it was no surprise that he was viewed as a heathen and an infidel by his family when he refused to be married in the church.*

lilliputian (lil·i·ˈpyoo·shăn) *adj.* 1. very small, tiny. 2. trivial or petty. *My troubles are lilliputian compared to hers, and I am thankful that I do not have such major issues in my life.*

mercurial (měr·ˈkyoor·i·ăl) *adj.* 1. liable to change moods suddenly. 2. lively, changeable, volatile. *Fiona is so mercurial that you never know what kind of reaction to expect.*

narcissism (ˈnarh·si·siz·ĕm) *n.* admiration or worship of oneself; excessive interest in one's own personal features. *Some critics say that movie stars are guilty of narcissism.*

occult (ŏ·ˈkult) *adj.* 1. secret, hidden, concealed. 2. involving the realm of the supernatural. 3. beyond ordinary understanding, incomprehensible. *The rights and beliefs of the occult organization were finally made a matter of public record after a long investigation.*

omnipotent (om·ˈnip·ŏ·tĕnt) *adj.* having unlimited or universal power or force. *In Greek mythology, Zeus was the most powerful god, but he was not omnipotent, since even his rule was often held in check by the unchangeable laws of the Three Fates.*

omniscient (om·ˈnish·ĕnt) *adj.* having infinite knowledge; knowing all things. *In a story with an omniscient narrator, we can hear the thoughts and feelings of all of the characters.*

phoenix (ˈfee·niks) *n.* 1. a person or thing of unmatched beauty or excellence. 2. a person or thing that has become renewed or restored after suffering calamity or apparent annihilation (after the mythological bird that periodically immolated itself and rose from the ashes as a new phoenix). *The phoenix is often used to symbolize something that is indomitable or immortal.*

protean (ˈproh·tee·ăn) *adj.* taking many forms, changeable; variable, versatile. *In Native American mythology, the coyote is often called the "shape shifter" because he is such a protean character.*

sacrilegious (sak·rĭ·ˈleej·ŭs) *adj.* disrespectful or irreverent towards something regarded as sacred. *Her book was criticized by the church for being sacrilegious.*

For questions 441–448, in Column A you will find brief descriptions of the stories or mythological characters that are the source of the vocabulary words in Column B. Draw a line to match each vocabulary word to its source. (If you do not own this book, please write your answers on a separate piece of paper.)

Column A

Column B

441. From Jonathan Swift's *Gulliver's Travels*, when Gulliver travels to the land inhabited by people only six inches tall.

draconian

442. After the god in Greek mythology who had wings on his feet and moved very swiftly.

gargantuan

443. After the character in Greek mythology who was in love with his own reflection.

lilliputian

444. From a sixteenth-century tale by Francois Rabelais about the life of a giant.

mercurial

445. After the mythological bird that periodically ignites itself and arises anew from the fire.

narcissism

446. After the Greek god who had the power to change his shape at will.

phoenix

447. After the chivalrous, romantic, idealistic knight created by the early seventeenth-century Spanish writer Miguel de Cervantes.

protean

448. After the Athenian lawmaker who created a code of laws that punished people very severely even for minor offenses.

quixotic

For numbers 449–460, read the sentences below carefully. Choose the vocabulary word from the list below that best completes the sentence. Write the correct answer in the blank. (If you do not own this book, please write your answers on a separate piece of paper.)

apostate	imprecation
apotheosis	infidel
blasphemy	occult
desecrate	omnipotent
dogma	omniscient
hallow	sacrilegious

449. In this tale, the young wizard had to battle the evil sorcerer to destroy his _____ powers and free the world from his total rule.

450. Although he had been a believer for many years, Anthony became a(n) _____ after the church scandals shook the foundation of his faith.

451. Because Zeus was not a(n) _____ god, he did not know which of his sons would dethrone him.

452. Despite common belief, most modern-day witches do not really believe in the _____; rather, they practice a deep reverence for the earth and the innate spirit of all living things.

453. The main goal of Sunday school is to teach children the _____ of the church.

454. Salman Rushdie's prize-winning novel *The Satanic Verses* was considered so _____ by authorities that he had to leave his native Iran.

455. The vandals _____(ed) the holy shrine by covering it with spray paint.

456. Long a(n) _____, Joshua decided to give religion a try when he fell in love with a woman who was deeply faithful.

457. In the fairy tale, the witch's _____ turned the poor shepherd into a toad.

458. In the wedding ceremony, the priest offered a special blessing over the bride and groom to _____ their union before God.

459. The sociologist argued that the _____ of film stars and athletes is to be expected in a culture that is not firmly grounded in religion.

460. The church accused Galileo of _____ when he claimed that the Earth revolved around the sun and that the Earth (and therefore human beings) was not the center of the universe.

Answers

441. *Lilliputian* means very small, tiny; trivial or petty. The land was called Lilliput.

442. *Mercurial* means liable to change moods suddenly; lively, changeable, volatile. The Greek god was Mercury.

443. *Narcissism* is admiration or worship of oneself; excessive interest in one's own personal features. The mythological character was Narcissus.

444. *Gargantuan* means gigantic, huge. The gigantic character was Gargantua.

445. A *phoenix* is a person or thing of unmatched beauty or excellence; a person or thing that has become renewed or restored after suffering calamity or apparent annihilation.

446. *Protean* means taking many forms; changeable, variable. The Greek god was Proteus.

447. *Quixotic* means extravagantly chivalrous and unselfish; romantically idealistic, impractical. Cervantes' hero was Don Quixote.

448. *Draconian* means very harsh, extremely severe. The lawmaker was Draco.

449. *Omnipotent* means having unlimited or universal power or force.

450. An *apostate* is someone who abandons long-held religious or political beliefs.

451. *Omniscient* means having infinite knowledge; knowing all things.

452. *Occult* means secret, hidden; involving the realm of the supernatural; incomprehensible.

453. *Dogma* is a system of principles or beliefs; a prescribed doctrine.

454. *Sacrilegious* means disrespectful or irreverent towards something regarded as sacred.

455. To *desecrate* is to violate the sacredness of something; to profane.

456. An *infidel* is a non-believer, a person with no religious beliefs, or one who does not accept a particular doctrine or system of beliefs.

457. An *imprecation* is a curse.

458. To *hallow* is to make holy, to consecrate.

459. An *apotheosis* is a deification, an exalted or glorified ideal.

460. *Blasphemy* is a contemptuous or irreverent act, utterance, attitude, or writing against God or other things considered sacred.

24

Ways of Being— More Words to Describe People and Their Behavior

Are you a *pragmatic* person who likes to be as practical as possible? Do you know a *hapless* person who always seems to be having bad luck? The 20 words in this chapter offer more ways to describe people and the ways they behave. You can find the answers to each question in this section at the end of the chapter.

Word List

baleful (ˈbayl·fŭl) *adj.* harmful, menacing, destructive, sinister. *Whether it's a man, woman, car, or animal, you can be certain to find at least one baleful character in a Stephen King horror novel.*

demure (di·ˈmyoor) *adj.* modest and shy, or pretending to be so. *When it was to her advantage, Sharon could be very demure, but otherwise she was quite outgoing.*

eminent (ˈem·ĭ·něnt) *adj.* towering above or more prominent than others, lofty; standing above others in quality, character, reputation, etc.; distinguished. *The chairperson proudly announced that the keynote speaker at the animal rights convention would be the eminent primatologist Jane Goodall.*

erratic (i·ˈrat·ik) *adj.* 1. moving or behaving in an irregular, uneven, or inconsistent manner. 2. deviating from the normal or typical course of action, opinion, etc. *During an earthquake, a seismograph's needle moves in an erratic manner.*

hapless (ˈhap·lis) *adj.* unlucky, unfortunate. *The hapless circumstances of her journey resulted in lost luggage, missed connections, and a very late arrival.*

ignominious (ig·nŏ·ˈmin·i·ŭs) *adj.* 1. marked by shame or disgrace. 2. deserving disgrace or shame; despicable. *The evidence of plagiarism brought an ignominious end to what had been a notable career for the talented young author.*

implacable (im·ˈplak·ă·běl) *adj.* incapable of being placated or appeased; inexorable. *Some of the people who call the customer service desk for assistance are implacable, but most are relatively easy to serve.*

indefatigable (in·di·ˈfat·ĭ·gă·běl) *adj.* not easily exhausted or fatigued; tireless. *The indefatigability of the suffragette movement led to the passage of the Twentieth Amendment, guaranteeing women the right to vote.*

indomitable (in·ˈdom·i·tă·běl) *adj.* not able to be vanquished or overcome, unconquerable; not easily discouraged or subdued. *The indomitable spirit of the Olympic athletes was inspirational.*

inimitable (i·ˈnim·i·tă·běl) *adj.* defying imitation, unmatchable. *His performance on the tennis court was inimitable, and he won three championships.*

intransigent (in·ˈtran·si·jěnt) *adj.* unwilling to compromise, stubborn. *Young children can be intransigent when it comes to what foods they will eat, insisting on familiar favorites and rejecting anything new.*

obdurate (′ob·dŭ·rit) *adj.* stubborn and inflexible; hardhearted, not easily moved to pity. *I doubt he will change his mind; he's the most obdurate person I know.*

pragmatic (prag·′mat·′ik) *adj.* practical, matter-of-fact; favoring utility. *Since we don't have money or time to waste, I think we should take the most pragmatic approach.*

refractory (ri·′frak·tŏ·ree) *adj.* stubborn, unmanageable; resisting control or discipline. *Elena is a counselor for refractory children in an alternative school setting.*

renowned (ri·′nownd) *adj.* famous; widely known and esteemed. *The renowned historian, Stephen Ambrose, wrote many books that were popular both with scholars and the general public.*

scurvy (′skur·vee) *adj.* contemptible, mean. *That scurvy knave has ruined my plans again.*

sublime (sŭ·′blīm) *adj.* having noble or majestic qualities; inspiring awe, adoration, or reverence; lofty, supreme. *Beethoven's music is simply sublime.*

svelte (svelt) *adj.* slender and graceful, suave. *The svelte actress glided around the room in her elegant gown.*

untoward (un·′tohrd) *adj.* 1. contrary to one's best interest or welfare; inconvenient, troublesome; adverse. 2. improper, unseemly, or perverse. *Jackson's untoward remarks made Amelia very uncomfortable.*

volatile (′vol·ă·til) *adj.* 1. varying widely; inconstant, changeable, or fickle. 2. unstable, explosive, likely to change suddenly or violently. 3. (in chemistry) evaporating readily. *Dan's volatile personality has been compared to that of Dr. Jekyll and Mr. Hyde.*

For questions 461–470, read the sentences below carefully. Decide which vocabulary word best describes the person or behavior described. Circle the correct answer. (If you do not own this book, please write your answers on a separate piece of paper.)

461. Kayla hasn't been her usual self since the accident; she often says and does things she wouldn't normally say or do.
   a. pragmatic
   b. erratic
   c. sublime
   d. baleful

462. Dr. Nash is the most successful and respected neurologist in the country.
   a. indefatigable
   b. obdurate
   c. demure
   d. eminent

463. No matter how much his management team begged him, Mr. Edwards refused to consider Sampson's proposal.
   a. baleful
   b. implacable
   c. obdurate
   d. pragmatic

464. No matter what Norton did, bad luck seemed to follow him wherever he went.
   a. implacable
   b. ignominious
   c. scurvy
   d. eminent

465. Godfrey was a liar and a thief, and only time would tell if he could turn his life around.
   a. baleful
   b. intransigent
   c. indomitable
   d. untoward

466. People were careful with what they said to Seymour, for his temper was likely to flare at the slightest provocation.
a. eminent
b. hapless
c. volatile
d. sublime

467. Last year's Woodson High School debate team could not be beaten, not even by its chief rival, the four-time state champions from Jacksonville High.
a. indomitable
b. refractory
c. renowned
d. implacable

468. The composer's new opera was so beautiful and majestic that it won the adoration of even the toughest critics.
a. erratic
b. obdurate
c. inimitable
d. sublime

469. The child refused to listen to the babysitter and insisted that she would *not* go to bed until her parents came home.
a. indomitable
b. refractory
c. pragmatic
d. volatile

470. No matter what his parents said, the spoiled child would not stop crying because he did not get the gift he wanted.
a. obdurate
b. eminent
c. implacable
d. baleful

For questions 471–480, draw a line to match the vocabulary word in Column A with its synonym in Column B. (If you do not own this book, please write your answers on a separate piece of paper.)

Column A	Column B
471. demure	contemptible
472. ignominious	despicable
473. indefatigable	famous
474. inimitable	improper
475. intransigent	modest
476. pragmatic	practical
477. renowned	stubborn
478. scurvy	suave
479. svelte	tireless
480. untoward	unique

Answers

461. **b.** *Erratic* means moving or behaving in an irregular, uneven, or inconsistent manner; deviating from the normal or typical course, opinion, etc.

462. **d.** *Eminent* means standing above others in quality, character, reputation, etc.; distinguished; towering above or more prominent than others.

463. **c.** *Obdurate* means stubborn and inflexible; hardhearted, not easily moved to pity.

464. **d.** *Hapless* means unlucky, unfortunate.

465. **a.** A *baleful* person is harmful, menacing, destructive; sinister.

466. **c.** *Volatile* means unstable, explosive, likely to change suddenly or violently. It also means varying widely; inconsistent, changeable, fickle.

467. **a.** *Indomitable* means unconquerable, not easily subdued.

468. **d.** Something *sublime* has noble or majestic qualities and inspires awe, adoration, or reverence.

469. **b.** *Refractory* means stubborn; unmanageable, resisting control or discipline.

470. **c.** *Implacable* means incapable of being placated or appeased.

471. *modest. Demure* means modest and shy, or pretending to be so.

472. *despicable. Ignominious* means marked by shame or disgrace; deserving disgrace or shame, despicable.

473. *tireless. Indefatigable* means not easily exhausted or fatigued; tireless.

474. *unique. Inimitable* means defying imitation; unmatchable.

475. *stubborn. Intransigent* means unwilling to compromise, stubborn.

476. *practical. Pragmatic* means practical, matter-of-fact, favoring utility.

477. *famous. Renowned* means famous; widely known and esteemed.

478. *contemptible. Scurvy* means contemptible; mean.

479. *suave. Svelte* means slender and graceful; suave.

480. *improper. Untoward* means improper, unseemly, perverse. It also means contrary to one's best interest or welfare; adverse.

25

Vocabulary Grab Bag

Did you know that Chapter 24 was the *penultimate* chapter of this book? Now that you have added a *bevy* of new words to you vocabulary, you are ready to tackle the last chapter. These final 21 words offer a grab bag of useful terms. You can find the answers to each question in this section at the end of the chapter.

Word List

addle ('ad·ĕl) *v.* 1. to muddle or confuse. 2. to become rotten, as in an egg. *The jury found the defendant addled at the end of the prosecuting attorney's questions.*

apex ('ay·peks) *n.* 1. the highest point. 2. tip, pointed end. *Upon reaching the apex of the mountain, the climbers placed their flag in the snow.*

approbation (ap·rŏ·'bay·shŏn) *n.* approval. *The local authorities issued an approbation to close the street for a festival on St. Patrick's Day.*

auspice ('aw·spis) *n.* 1. protection or support, patronage. 2. a forecast or omen. *The children's art museum was able to continue operating through the auspices of an anonymous wealthy benefactor.*

bevy ('bev·ee) *n.* 1. a large group or assemblage. 2. a flock of animals or birds. *There was a lively bevy of eager bingo fans waiting outside the bingo hall for the game to begin.*

de facto (dee 'fak·toh) in reality or fact; actual. *Though there was a ceremonial head of government, General Ashtononi was the de facto leader of the country.*

denouement (day·noo·'mahn) *n.* the resolution or clearing up of the plot at the end of a narrative; the outcome or solution of an often complex series of events. *The students sat at the edge of their seats as they listened to the denouement of the story.*

elite (i·'leet) *n.* 1. the best or most skilled members of a social group or class. 2. a person or group regarded as superior. *Within the student orchestra, there existed a small group of musical elite who performed around the country.*

engender (en·'jen·dĕr) *v.* to produce, give rise to; bring into existence. *Professor Sorenson's support worked to engender Samantha's desire to pursue a Ph.D.*

inured (in·'yoord) *adj.* accustomed to, adapted. *Trisha had become inured to her boss's criticism, so it no longer bothered her.*

mendacity (men·'das·i·tee) *n.* 1. the tendency to be dishonest or untruthful. 2. a falsehood or lie. *Carlos's mendacity has made him very unpopular with his classmates, who don't feel they can trust him.*

obviate ('ob·vi·ayt) *v.* to make unnecessary, get rid of. *Hiring Magdalena would obviate the need to hire a music tutor, for she is also a classical pianist.*

penultimate (pi·'nul·tī·mit) *adj.* next to last. *There's a real surprise for the audience in the penultimate scene.*

schism ('siz·ĕm) *n.* a separation or division into factions because of a difference in belief or opinion. *The schism between the two parties was forgotten as they united around a common cause.*

semantics (si·'man·tiks) *n.* 1. the study of meaning in language. 2. the meaning, connotation, or interpretation of words, symbols, or other forms. 3. the study of relationships between signs or symbols and their meanings. *He claims it's a matter of semantics, but the matter is not open to interpretation.*

simian ('sim·i·ăn) *adj.* of or like an ape or monkey. *Creationists do not believe that humans have simian ancestors.*

sophistry ('sof·i·stree) *n.* clever but faulty reasoning; a plausible but invalid argument intended to deceive by appearing sound. *I was amused by his sophistry but knew he had a little more research to do before he presented his argument to the distinguished scholars in his field.*

supplicant ('sup·lĭ·kănt) *n.* a person who asks humbly for something; one who beseeches or entreats. *The supplicants begged for forgiveness.*

temerity (tĕ·'mer·i·tee) *n.* foolish disregard of danger; brashness, audacity. *This is no time for temerity; we must move cautiously to avoid any further damage.*

tenet ('ten·it) *n.* a belief, opinion, doctrine, or principle held to be true by a person, group, or organization. *This pamphlet describes the tenets of Amnesty International.*

undulate ('un·jŭ·layt) *v.* to move in waves or in a wavelike fashion; fluctuate. *The curtains undulated in the breeze.*

For numbers 481–501, read the sentences or questions below carefully. Decide which answer best describes the vocabulary word or answers the question in the prompt. Circle the correct answer. (If you do not own this book, please write your answers on a separate piece of paper.)

481. A person who studies *semantics* studies
   a. the history of language.
   b. the meaning and interpretation of words and symbols.
   c. extinct languages.
   d. the use of symbols to solve mathematical problems.

482. The *penultimate* chapter in a book is
   a. the first chapter.
   b. the middle chapter.
   c. the second to last chapter.
   d. the last chapter.

483. If you are at the *apex* of your career, you are
   a. just starting out.
   b. about to switch to a new field.
   c. just about to quit.
   d. at the height of your career.

484. A politician who has a *bevy* of supporters
   a. has only a few supporters.
   b. has a large group of supporters.
   c. has supporters who contribute large amounts of money.
   d. has supporters who are very nice.

485. The *denouement* of a movie would most likely occur
   a. in the first five minutes.
   b. in the middle of the film.
   c. in the last ten minutes.
   d. in advertisements.

486. If you *engender* mistrust between two coworkers, you
   a. create that mistrust.
   b. remove that mistrust.
   c. worsen that mistrust.
   d. understand that mistrust.

487. Which of the following is a *supplicant*?
  a. an employee asking for a raise
  b. a prisoner of war begging for mercy
  c. a person applying for a job
  d. a supplier of goods or services

488. An experiment performed on a *simian* would be performed on
  a. a human being.
  b. a volunteer.
  c. a monkey.
  d. rabbit.

489. A person who is known for his *mendacity* can be expected to
  a. always tell the truth.
  b. be a great story teller.
  c. be very persistent.
  d. be dishonest.

490. Which of the following would you expect to *undulate*?
  a. a flag
  b. an airplane
  c. a dog
  d. a teacher

491. If you *addle* someone while he or she is talking, you
  a. listen carefully to that person.
  b. confuse that person.
  c. ignore that person.
  d. look that person in the eye.

492. A person who is under the *auspices* of someone else is
  a. estranged from the other person.
  b. a close family member.
  c. beyond that person's comprehension.
  d. being protected or supported by that person.

493. If you give someone your *approbation*, you give them
  a. your support.
  b. your approval.
  c. your love.
  d. your notice of resignation.

494. In which case is the assistant the *de facto* boss?
a. when the assistant is the one who makes all of the decisions
b. when the assistant has been promoted to the boss's position
c. when the assistant has so much work that he or she has to hire his or her own assistant
d. when the assistant starts his or her own company

495. When married couples have become *inured* to each other, they have
a. become tired of each other.
b. become indebted to each other.
c. become used to each other.
d. become insensitive to each other.

496. A *schism* between two people is a(n)
a. agreement.
b. argument.
c. closeness because of many shared beliefs.
d. separation because of a difference of opinion.

497. Which of the following is a *tenet* of the United States of America?
a. Puerto Rico
b. freedom of speech
c. Mexico
d. trial by jury

498. If you are guilty of *temerity*, you have done something
a. wasteful.
b. illegal.
c. brash.
d. sacrilegious.

499. Which of the following would be considered *elite* in the military?
a. a foot soldier
b. an army medic
c. a Green Beret
d. a platoon leader

500. Where are you most likely to find an example of *sophistry*?
   a. during a debate between political candidates
   b. during a formal dinner during the holidays
   c. during a concert
   d. at the end of a mystery novel

501. Which of the following will *obviate* your need for this book?
   a. failing to answer most of the questions correctly
   b. loaning it to a friend
   c. preparing for a standardized test like the SAT exam
   d. incorporating all of these words into your vocabulary

Answers

481. **b.** *Semantics* is the study of meaning in language; the study of relationships between signs and symbols and their meanings.

482. **c.** *Penultimate* means next to last.

483. **d.** *Apex* is the highest point; tip or pointed end.

484. **b.** A *bevy* is a large group or assemblage. It also means a flock of animals or birds.

485. **c.** The *denouement* is the resolution or clearing up of the plot at the end of a narrative.

486. **a.** To *engender* is to produce; to give rise to, bring into existence.

487. **b.** A *supplicant* is someone who beseeches or entreats; someone who asks humbly for something.

488. **c.** *Simian* is of, or like, an ape or monkey.

489. **d.** *Mendacity* is the tendency to be dishonest or untruthful; a falsehood or lie.

490. **a.** To *undulate* is to move in waves or in a wavelike fashion.

491. **b.** To *addle* means to muddle or confuse. It also means to become rotten, as in an egg.

492. **d.** *Auspice* means protection or support; patronage. It also means a forecast or omen.

493. **b.** *Approbation* means approval.

494. **a.** *De facto* means in reality or fact; actual.

495. **c.** *Inured* means accustomed to; adapted.

496. **d.** A *schism* is a separation or division into factions because of a difference in belief or opinion.

497. **b.** A *tenet* is a belief, opinion, doctrine, or principle held to be true by a person, group, or organization.

498. **c.** *Temerity* is the foolish disregard of danger; brashness, audacity.

499. **c.** *Elite* means the best or most skilled members of a social group or class; a person or group regarded as superior.

500. **a.** *Sophistry* is clever but faulty reasoning; a plausible but invalid argument intended to deceive by appearing sound.

501. **d.** To *obviate* is to make unnecessary, to get rid of.

Congratulations! You've tackled 501 vocabulary questions and added dozens of new words to your vocabulary. Remember, the best way to keep these words in your vocabulary is to *use them*. Start now! Review the vocabulary list and these lessons periodically to refresh your memory.

Want to expand your vocabulary even more? Start a vocabulary list of your own. Write down unfamiliar words that you come across throughout the day. Look up the meanings and pronunciations and copy them down. Write your own sentences using these words to lock their meaning in your memory. Once you collect a dozen or so words, create your own exercises like those in this book. Use your new vocabulary words as often as possible to keep them fresh in your memory.

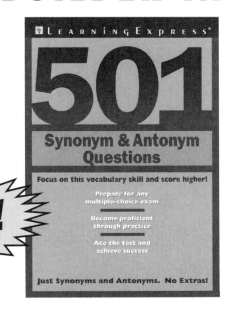